A Definitive Guide to

2020 IPAD PRO

For The Elderly

Essential Tips and Tricks to Apple's 4th Generation iPad Pro for Seniors

DERRICK

RICHARD

Copyright

Derrick Richard

ISBN: 9798634697444

USA | UK | Canada

Printed on acid-free paper.

Table of Contents

Chapter 4

Chapter 5

Why This Guide?

You just got the 2020 iPad Pro and as a senior, you need a guide to walk you through the essential settings, configurations, New iPadOS 13.4 and numerous handy tips, tricks, essential features and various troubleshooting techniques, then this guide is for you. It provides an insight into the basic functions of the 4th Generation iPad pro such as FaceID, Airdrop, Screen Time, Side Car etc to advanced functions such as creating Siri shortcuts, advanced gestures, setting up advanced security, Augumented Reality, voice control for the iPad and techniques to master various advanced settings to safeguard your device and increase the productivity of your device.

The book also provides seamless techniques to connect your iPad pro to several hardware devices such as the magic mouse, keyboard, trackpad, external monitors, Hyperdrive, Airfly, Gopro, Xbox Console, PS4 Console and several advanced hacks that would push your 2020 iPad Pro to its maximum performance.

Chapter 1

Evolution of the Apple iPad From 2010 to 2020

To appreciate how far the Apple iPad has evolved, we will take a short trip down memory lane from the first iPad (first generation iPad 1) which was introduced to the public in April 2010 to the iPad Pro (2nd Generation) launched in September 2018.

iPad

The first ever iPad was announced on the 27th of January 2010 by Steve Jobs at a media conference in San Francisco. There was a wide acceptance for this device leading to sales of three million units in the first 80 days after it was launched. This was a huge success and marked the begining of the iPad series.

The iPad has a display screen 9.7 inches (1024 x 768), RAM speed of 256 MB running on iOS 3.2 operating system powered by Apple A4 chip.

The iPad was revolutionary at the time; it could play music, send and receive emails and surf the web. It also has gaming apps, had access to GPS and social media apps all on a compact portable slate. At introduction, the iPad received several positive reviews from various tech blogs and publishers. The reviews praised the device for its wide range of capabilities and labeled it as a competitor to most laptops and netbooks.

iPad 2

At the launch of the iPad 2 in March 2011, Apple sold more than 15 million units. The tablet was 33% thinner than its predecessor and 15% lighter. The iPad 2 came with a much more better processor which was twice as fast as the original iPad and it also boasts of a GPU operation speed nine times faster than the original iPad. It has a display screen of 9.7 inches (1024 x 768) with a Ram speed of 512MB. The system software was upgraded to iOS 4.3 powered by the Apple A5 CPU which is an upgrade from the Apple A4 chip present in the original iPad. The iPad 2 was the first iPad to feature a Visual Graphics Array (VGA) front-facing camera and a 720p rear-facing camera. The iPad 2 was available in three storage sizes of 16, 32 and 64GB, black and white and each having a white front glass panel.

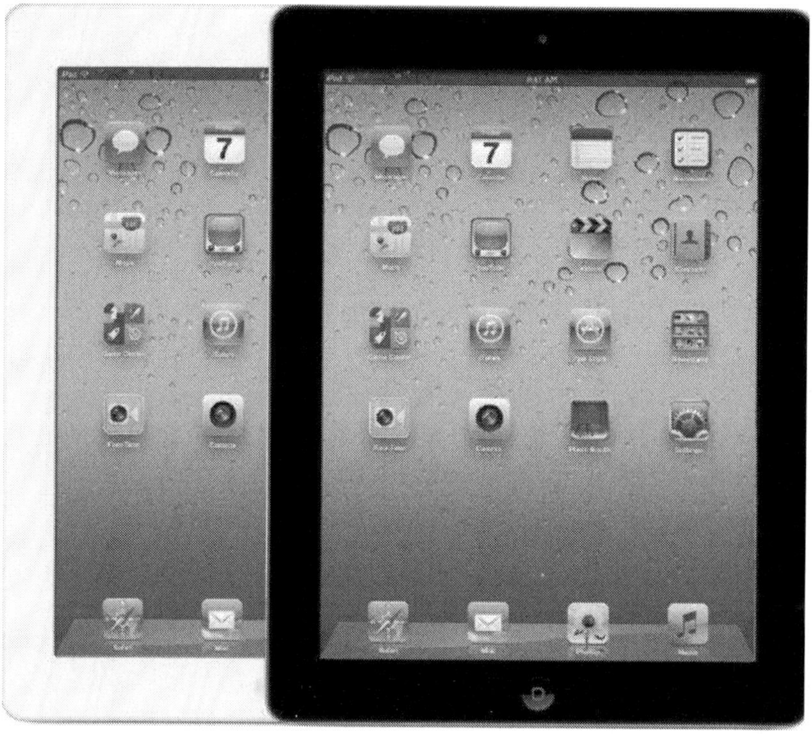

Image of iPad 2

Although the iPad 2 was praised for its hardware improvement (the new A5 chip), it received mixed perception from tech blogs and publishers for its closed and proprietary nature of iOS.

iPad 3

The third-generation iPad was released in March 2012 and it received a lot of positive reviews for its retina display, camera, processor and LTE support. The iPad 3 sold 3 million units in the first three days claiming 69.6 percent of the global tablet market in the second quarter of 2012. It boasts of a 9.7 inches display screen (2048 x 1536), an Apple A5X chip and a 1GB RAM speed.

Image of iPad 3

The iPad 3 operating system was upgraded to iOS 5.1 and it became the first iPad with a Retina Display which boosted the screen resolution. It was adjudged to have the most spectacular display seen on a mobile device. In addition to its brilliant display, Apple Added a 5MP camera, 1080p video recording.

iPad 4

The iPad 4 which is the fourth generation of iPads was introduced in November 2012. The device maintained the retina display but featured an upgraded chip - the Apple A6X and the operating system was upgraded to iOS 6. The RAM and the display screen was maintained at 1GB and 9.7 inches (2048 x 1536) respectively. The iPad 4 got several positive reviews for its hardware improvements as well as the retina display.

iPad Mini

The first generation iPad Mini was launched alongside the iPad 4 in November 2012. The iPad mini came with a smaller screen and was aimed to compete with smaller tablets such as Amazon's Kindle Fire and Nexus 7. It has a screen 7.9 inches and like the iPad 2, it was powered by an Apple A5 chip. It has a RAM speed of 512MB and the iOS 6 operating system.

Reviews for the iPad miniowere positive and the focus was on the size, design and the introduction of more applications. Three million units were sold in the first weekend of release.

iPad Air

The iPad Air which was released into the market in November 2013 marked the first major design change by Apple since the introduction of iPad in 2010. iPad Air had a thinner design that is, 7.5mm thick and it has a smaller bezel. A new faster 64-bit processor chip was also introduced in the iPad air called Apple A7. The RAM speed was kept at 1 GB with the operating system upgraded to iOS 7. The display size was left at 7.9 inches and a significantly improved front-facing and a rear camera were introduced.

The iPad Air's launch was greeted with significantly high positive reviews due to its performance, crisp and colorful retina display plus a reduced weight and size.

iPad Mini 2

The iPad Mini 2 was released alongside iPad Air in November 2013. It boasts of an improved retina display, Apple A7 chip, 1 GB RAM speed and an iOS 7 operating system. The iPad Mini 2 had positive reviews from tech bloggers because it has the same hardware features as the iPad Air, yet is significantly lighter.

iPad Air 2

Apple released the iPad Air 2 in October 2014 and it was embraced with a lot of positive reviews. The iPad Air 2 is thinner and with the introduction of a 2GB RAM, the speed significantly improved when compared to the older generation of iPads. It came with a chip known as the Apple 8X and upgraded operating software (iOS 8.1). It also features a fingerprint Touch ID sensor and it is the first iOS device to feature a triple core CPU.

iPad Mini 3

The iPad Mini 3 was introduced into the market alongside iPad Air 2. The iPad Mini 3 has all the features of the iPad mini 2 in design and hardware configuration but Touch ID was added to the iPad mini 3 and this differentiates it from the iPad Mini 2.

iPad Pro 12.9

The iPad Pro was announced in September 2015. It came with a huge screen (12.9

inches), a 4GB RAM which increased the speed, and it operates on the iOS 9.1 Operating System. It also came with a new A9X CPU which is faster than the original iPad Air. Apple promoted the iPad Pro as a replacement for PC, but reviewers were of a different opinion.

iPad Mini 4

The suffix "4" indicate 4th generation. The iPad Mini 4th generation was announced along side the iPad Pro in September 9, 2015. It is the first major redesign of the iPad mini series. It is thinner, lighter and taller than previous versions. The iPad Mini 4 featured hardware closer in specification to that of the iPad Air 2. It boasts of a dual-core Apple A8 chip, a 2GB RAM which makes multitasking seamless and a display screen of 7.9 inches. The Operating System for the iPad mini 4 is iOS 9.0.

First Generation iPad Pro 9.7

The iPad Pro 9.7 was announced in March 2016. It is a smaller version of the iPad Pro with a 2GB RAM, an Apple A9X chip and iOS 9.3 Operating System.

It has a 9.7 inches display screen.

iPad 5th Generation

iPad 5 or 5th Generation iPad was launched in March 2017. Apple designed the iPad 5 with affordability in mind. However, it received a mixed reaction at launch. While most tech reviewers hailed its affordability and speed, others criticized it for two major reasons - the absence of anti-reflective coating and lack of fully laminated display. The iPad 5 runs on the Apple A9 chip and the iOS 10.2 Operating System.

2nd Generation iPad Pro 10.5/12.9

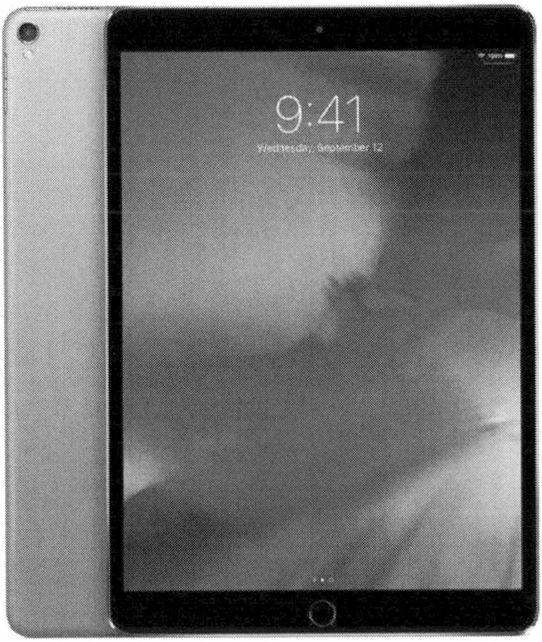

The iPad Pro 2 was released in June 2017. It came in two display sizes - 10.5 inches and 12.9 inches. The specifications include Apple A10X chip, 4GB RAM and an iOS 10.3 Operating System. The iPad Pro 2 was adjudged to have the highest storage capacity (512 GB) of any iOS device at launch. Its picture quality was also adjudged the best of any iPad before it, with a 7MP and 12-Mega-pixel front-facing and rear-facing camera respectively.

iPad 6th Generation

The iPad 6th Generation was announced in March 2018. It came with the Apple A10 processor, a 2GB RAM and iOS 11 Operating System. iPad 6 was the first iPad to support Apple Pencil. It has a display screen of 9.7 inches (1536 x 2048).

iPad Mini 5

The iPad Mini 5 comes in 64GB or 256GB storage. It has a fully laminated 7.9-inch retina display with a resolution of 2048 x 1536 at 326ppi. The iPad 5 has a P3 wide color gamut true-tone Oleophobic and anti-reflective Coating which has up to 500 nits of brightness. Around the outside edge of the iPad Mini 5 is the stereo speakers at the bottom, a lightning port, at the side the Volume up/down buttons and at the top, the Power/Sleep/Wake button, a little microphone and a headphone jack. At the rear, a microphone and an 8 Megapixel (f/2.4) autofocus camera which does 1080P video. At the front of the iPad Mini 5 is a 7MP (f/2.2) front-facing camera that also does 1080P videos. iPad Mini 5 is compatible with the first Generation Apple Pencil.

2018 iPad Pro (3rd Generation)

iPad Pro 11" & 12.9" were released in November 2018. It is a shift from previous versions and generations of iPads. It was unlike any iPad that Apple has produced in the past. Apple likened the iPad Pro to a computer. The 3rd Generation iPad Pro came with an A12X Bionic. Which was adjudged the fastest processor at that time.

Chapter 2

2020 iPad Pro (4th Generation)

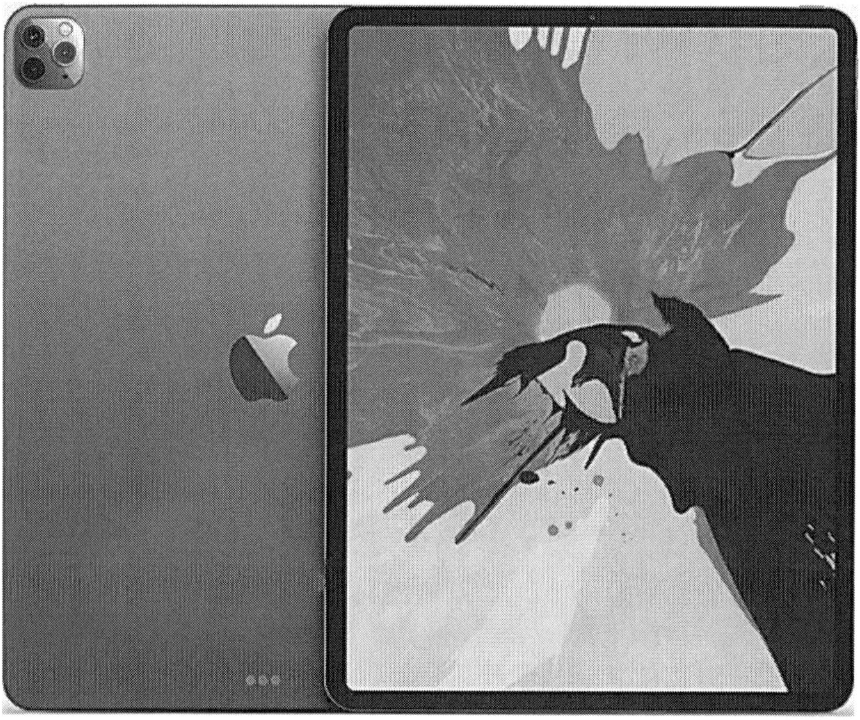

The 4th Generation iPad Pro introduced in March 2020 came in two sizes, the 11" and the 12.9" model with silver or space gray color options. It is dubbed "a performance monster" and the ideal iPad for gaming, multitasking and heavy-duty performance. The front of the 2020

iPad Pro looks pretty much the same as the 2018 iPad Pro. The difference, however, is at the back with the dual camera of the 2020 iPad Pro. Apple also carried out a lot of updates in terms of software. The iPad Pro's processor is upgraded from the A12X Bionic of the 3rd Generation to the new A12Z Bionic and 8 core graphic processor making this iPad the fastest tablet in terms of processing speed and longer sustained performance. This chip is powerful enough for seamless graphics designs using Photoshop and video editing using the iMovie App on the iPad Pro. The A12Z Bionic chip makes the iPad pro 98% faster than most portable PCs. In addition to the processor, the 2020 iPad Pro come with an updated memory storage, which starts at 128GB. Other versions of the 4th generation iPad Pro come with 256GB, 512GB and 1TB of storage. Apple also made some improvements in the Wifi connectivity of the iPad pro, by adopting the new Wifi 6 80211ax as they did with the iPhone 11 line. This gives the 2020 iPad Pro a better performance in terms of wireless connectivity in congested networks. The 2020 iPad Pro has 6GB of RAM compared to the 4GB RAM of the 2018 model.

One of the significant additions to the 2020 iPad Pro is the introduction of the dual-camera system. In addition to the 12 MP Wide lens that is obtainable in the 3rd Generation iPad Pro, Apple added a second 10 Mega Pixel Ultra Wide lens, upgrading the iPad Pro to shoot 4K videos at 24fps, unlike the 2018 version that is limited to 30 and 60 fps.

In addition to the dual-camera system, Apple also added a Light Detection and Ranging (LiDAR) Scanning Sensor System. It is a remote sensing method that uses light in the form of a pulsed laser to measure distance to an object.

These light pulses generate accurate, high-resolution 3D information of the object. In other words, LiDAR is a time of flight sensor that allows for a better Artificial Intelligence and augmented reality Experience. For instance, users can take 3D images of a room with the LiDAR system suggesting a better placement of objects in the room or ideal furniture addition. It is also used for precision-based measurements on the measuring app. Note that LiDAR sensor(s) is used by most tech companies in self-driven cars. It is the best sensor out there for depth sensing and object tracking.

In addition, the 2020 iPad Pro also features a new cursor system on the screen to aid precision-based apps like spreadsheets and word processor users.

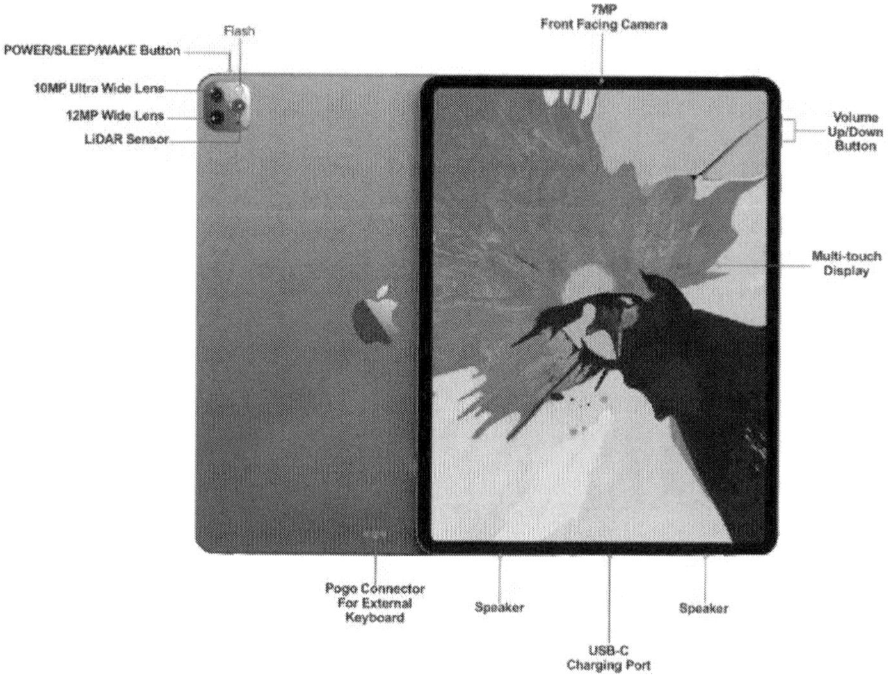

The 4th Generation iPad Pro's screen goes from edge to edge with a thin frame 5.9mm thin) and its liquid retina display (2732 x 2048) is one of the most advanced responsive display ever introduced to a tablet. The Display has a pixel density of 264ppi and also goes up to 600nits of brightness. The 2020 iPad Pro is redesigned to work in any orientation; hence there is no wrong way to place it. Also, multi-tasking is faster than ever on the iPad Pro.

At the back of the iPad Pro, there are a hundred and two magnets all precisely lined to create a system that holds the smart folio and the Magic keyboard folio. The Magic keyboard and the Apple pencil 2 snaps into place seamlessly at the back and side of the ipad pro respecitively. Drawing or writing with the Apple pencil feels natural; its symmetrical touch sensors give users more control, for instance, switching between tools with a double tap on the pen.

Other additions to the 2020 iPad Pro include four speakers audio, five studio quality microphone, which is great for FaceTime and Podcasting. In addition, the 2020 iPad Pro comes with a 7MP true depth front facing camera for portrait selfies and 1080p, 60fps video. The batteries on the iPad Pro is now 28.65 watts hours which gives users up to 10 hours of use when surfing the internet watching videos non stop.

At the top of the iPad Pro is the POWER/ SLEEP/WAKE button with two speakers and two microphones. On the left side, we have another microphone. On the right side are the VOLUME UP and DOWN buttons. Also, on the right side is the magnetic dock that allows users to attach and also charge the Apple Pencil. At the bott-om, we have two more speakers and a USB-C port for charging the device and also for file transfers. With the USB-C port, the 2020 iPad Pro can easily connect to a digital camera, iPhones, external monitors and hardware that has the USB-C port.

What Comes in the Box

When you purchase the 2020 iPad Pro, the following are what comes along in the box

- The iPad Pro

- A Quick Guide
- Apple Stickers
- 18 Watts power brick
- One metre long USB-C Cable

Features of the iPadOS 13.4 on the iPad Pro

Apple introduced the iPadOS 13.4 alongside the 2020 iPad Pro. In this section, we will take a look at some of the new features of the iPad-OS 13.4 powered 4th Generation iPad Pro.

iCloud Folder Sharing

With iPadOS 13.4, Apple finally added 'folder sharing with iCloud Drive'. To do this, go to the

'Files' App › press and hold the folder you want to share › on the pop-up menu that comes up, tap on 'Share.' Click on 'Add People.' The 'Add people' options allow you to share the folder to only people you invite or grant access to the folder. You can then give them links to access the folder. You could also change permissions for who could upload, download, view or make changes to these files and help you work collaboratively.

New Memoji Stickers Added

Apple updated the Memoji with more stickers in iPadOS 13.4. There are nine new memoji stickers added, including - smiling face with heart, hand-pressed together, party face, etc.

Mail Interface Updated

The mail app interface on iPadOS 13.4 received an upgrade, especially when it comes to multitasking. You can take you new message; slide it over into split view. You can be writing a message on one side and reading a mail on the other side or browsing your inbox. Like with the other stock applications, there are additional keyboard shortcuts for theomail app in iPadOS 13.4. There are also visible controls to delete, move, reply or compose a message. However, this is more of a big deal on the iPhone than the iPad. Besides, responses to encrypted emails are automatically encrypted when you have S/MIME configured. However, you may need to have this set on the server-side, so everything is encrypted.

App Store Update

The iPadOS 13.4 that comes with the 4th generation iPad pro have the app store updated. With the app store, developers now have the option to give users universal purchase support for apps across iPhone, iPad, iPod touch, Mac and Apple TV. What this means is that if you purchase an application, you can have it on your iPhone, iPad, iPod touch, Mac and Apple TV all for free. This also applies to Apple Arcade and any other app for one fee if the developer chooses to do allow that.

Arcade Games

The iPadOS 13.4 allow recently played Arcade games to be carried across different devices. This means you can start a game on one device and continue playing it across other Apple devices.

TV App

There is an update to the TV App on iPadOS 13.4. Apple added 'Family Sharing' as one of the features. With family sharing, several members of the family can now have access to watch movies and TV series on their device from one subscription. You can also have access to their purchased movies and they can see yours as well.

Additional Settings for TV App

We now have download options for Wi-Fi or cellular, if you are using a cellular version of the iPad Pro. Under the Wi-Fi Downloads option, you now have options to choose between High-Quality Downloads or Fast Downloads, depending on your internet speed. The same is also true for Wi-Fi streaming with options for High-Quality Streaming or Data Saver option. To check these options out, go to 'Settings > 'TV.'

AR Quick Look Support

The iPad Pro iPADOS 13.4 now has AR Quick Look supports audio playback in USDZ files. What this does is if you are using augmented reality to maybe look at furniture around or things like that, you now have the ability for a quick look for audio playback in the file itself (USDZ file).

Keyboard Layout

Apple added an on-screen keyboard layout for the iPad Pro 12.9" that now matches the smart keyboard. If you have the smart keyboard, you can now match the same layout with the on-screen keyboard on the iPad Pro. In addition to this, Apple updated the Swiss-German keyboard layout supported on iPad Pro 12.9". Apple also added predictive typing support for the Arabic keyboard. For the Japanse keyboard update on iPadOS 13.4, Apple added live conversation for both Zhuyin and Japanese transforms Zhuyin into the correct character without pressing the space bar to convert text or select candidates. Still, on the keyboard update, Apple improved the Burmese keyboard, so punctuation symbols are now accessible from numbers and symbols.

iPadOS 13.4 also features a floating keyboard that can be moved around on the screen. It allows users to get an iPhone sized keyboard so you can comfortably type with one hand. This makes typing so much easier on the iPad Pro. You can re-dock the keyboard by dragging it down to the bottom of the screen. To change the on screen keyboard to a floating keyboard, perform a two-finger pinch-in on the keyboard. Pinch-out to bring the keyboard back to normal size.

Home Screen Icons

One of the features of the 4th Generation iPad Pro is the Home Screen app icon layout; there is a 5" x 6" app icon layout for a total of thirty app icons on the home screen. When you combine these thirty app icons to the now eighteen apps available in the dock, you have a total of forty-eight apps on the Home screen.

Today View

When you Swipe right on the first page of the Home screen, you will notice a new "today view" feature redesigned for iPadOS 13.4 The "today view" has all your configured widgets. When you swipe to reveal "today view", all other app icons remain on the home screen; they are compressed to fit into the home screen alongside "today view" widgets. You can enable today view to display on the first home screen page without the need to swipe › scroll down on "today view" › tap on "Edit" button and ENABLE "always show todays view on the home screen while in landscape mode" › tap "DONE."

Multitasking

Multitasking is incredibly flexible with the 4th Generation iPad Pro. Users can invoke slide over apps from either side of the screen. You can also have multiple apps in slide over - tap and slide apps from the dock atop of each other. You can also switch between slide over apps by sliding across the home indicator at the base of each slide over app. To invoke the slide over switcher in order to view all slide over apps, swipe up on the home indicator. Slide over apps can be closed by swiping up on the app while the slide over switcher is open.

Apps Expose

Apps Expose is another new feature of the iPad Pro. It allows you to open all the windows associated with a single app across multiple spaces on the screen. Long press an app > tap on "All Windows" to open up App expose for that app. One of the things that make apps expose compelling is the little plus "+" sign at the upper-right corner. That plus button allows you to open a single window of an application and when you tap on "Show all windows, it will display all other instances of that app. The apps expose is compactible with Safari, reminders, notes app, third-party apps, etc.

Drag to Create Windows

You can drag to create windows on the 4th Generation iPad Pro. For instance, you can drag an email address to create a new mail app window and you can also drag a URL to create a new Safari app window next to the mail app window. You can also do same thing with notifications. For instance, if you receive notification for the mail app, you can simply drag that notification to create a split view instance.

Reduced Latency for Apple Pencil 2

There is reduced latency as low as nine milliseconds with the Apple Pencil 2 on the 2020 iPad Pro. In other words, using the Apple pencil feels more natural, whether it is for drawing or annotation. You will also find newly redesigned tool palettes with less flat textures, which is more skill morphic. Another significant change to the Apple Pencil in iPadOS 13.4 is that the opacity size on each tool is now listed horizontally instead of vertically like it was listed in previous iPadOS. So when you change the opacity value, you will see the numerical representation on each tool listed horizontally.

Pixel eraser tool for Apple Pencil

The eraser tool previously erases the entire stroke, but in iOS 13.4, you have the option to switch to a pixel eraser that allows you to erase pixel by pixel. Instead of having to delete the entire stroke, you can carry out a more precise erasing.

Ruler for Creating Straight lines

In the Pencil tool palette, we have the ruler for creating straight lines. The ruler can be adjusted to various degrees.

Color Palette button

There is also an updated color palette button in iPadOS 13.4. You will also notice that the "Undo/Redo" buttons are now part of the markup toolset. Previously, they were separated from the markup tools. You can also swipe the markup tools to the left or right, upper-left or upper-right corner to minimize it and swipe to the middle to open it up. You can swipe the markup tools to the left, right, top and bottom sides, to dock them.

Taking Screenshots

With iOS 13.4, you can take a screenshot with Apple Pencil by drawing with the pencil from the bottom left corner. Another feature for taking screenshots is the ability to snap to borders when cropping screenshots.

Peek and Quick Action Shortcuts

In iPadOS 13.4, you can invoke quick actions shortcuts from the home screen by long pressing on an eligible app icon.

Magic Mouse Connectivity

iPadOS 13.4 supports magic mouse connectivity. You can connect a mouse to the iPad Pro using Bluetooth. Go to settings › Bluetooth › power ON your Magic Mouse › Under Other devices, tap on the magic mouse 2 and this pairs your magic mouse.

Magic Trackpad Connection

iPadOS 13.4 supports Magic Trackpad Connectivity. The Magic Trackpad is connected to the 2020 iPad Pro through the same method as the magic mouse. Go to settings › Bluetooth › power ON your Trackpad and pair › Under 'Other devices,' tap on the system admistrator trackpad and this pairs your magic trackpad to the iPad Pro.

Connecting a third-Party Wireless Mouse to Your iPad

The 4th Generation iPad pro supports the use of third party Bluetooth mouse. To enable mouse support, go to Settings › tap "Accessibility" › scroll down and tap "Touch." On the top, you will find the option for "AssistiveTouch," Turn it ON. Once in AssistiveTouch, scroll down and tap "Device" › pair Bluetooth devices. The interaction with mouse support works a little bit differently from the way you would use it on a macOS or Windows supported PC. For instance, if you want to move around the Home screen, you hold down the left click and drag the mouse over. To scroll up/down on a page, hold-down on left-click and move the mouse up or down.

Ability to Create a New Folder from "Save to Files" share sheet Interface

The files app also got a huge upgrade in iPadOS 13.4. One of the notable features is the ability to create a new folder directly from the "Save" dialogue that opens up from the share sheet whenever you save to the files app. To do this, tap the "New folders" button > type your folder name > tap "save". Also, in the new app folder, you will find a new sort option along with name, date, size, kind etc. This enables users to sort files by names, date, size, kind etc. There is also a column view; if you tap the column view button; this allows you to browse files and nested folders with a high-resolution preview. Column view also gives you access to rich meta-data and execute quick actions such as rotate, markup, create a pdf etc on the file. The files app also allows you to filter your searches so you can search by recent files, icloud drive or current folder. Finally, there are plenty of keyboard shortcuts for Files found in the files app. You will find shortcuts that allow you to browse directly to certain folders, you can connect directly to a server and there is also a sort by keyboard shortcuts options.

External Drive Support

iPadOS 13.4 has external drive support; this means you can connect and have access to an external storage drive directly to the iPad Pro via a USB type-C cable. You can tap and drag files from the iPad Pro internal Storage to the external drive and vice versa.

Desktop-Class Browsing

One of the most significant improvements in iPadOS 13.4 is desktop-class browsing within Safari. Not only does Safari identify itself as a Mac, but Apple has given it a lot of TLC to make it perform much more like a desktop browser which means users can now surf certain websites like square space and Google Docs just as you will do on a desktop. There are also lots of new keyboard shortcuts for Safari. You can also combine a shortcut with taps on the screen. For instance, you can download a link by holding options and tap, or save a link to your reading list by holding shift and tap.

Full toolbar in Split View for Safari

If you put Safari in split view in previous iPadOS, it omits much of the toolbar, but in iPadOS 13.4, the full toolbar is displayed for both windows.

Photos App

The editing section of the photos app is amazing with iPadOS 13.4. User can now quickly turn effects ON/OFF, adjust effect intensity, edit videos nondestructively with filters, adjust the intensity of filters, using the crop, trim, flip and aspect ratio tools non-destructively within the native photos app. A High-Key Light portrait Mode effect which creates a classic look with a monochromatic subject on a white background is also a new feature of the iPadOS 13.4. Another new photos app feature for the iPadOS 13.4 is the ability to adjust portrait mode intensity. You can use the slider to move light closer to your subject to smoothen skin and sharpen the eyes or decrease the intensity of the light by moving it away from your subject for a more settled look. Under the crop tab of the photos app editor, you will also notice that the reset button at the top has a slightly diffe-rent look.

Reminder App

The reminder app got a completely redesign-ned interface in iPadOS 13.4 It has new smart filters, which allows users to filter by day, by schedule, by all, by flagged and several new keyboard shortcuts.

Side Car

Side car also got some improvement. Side car is a feature that allows you to use the iPad Pro as an external display. You can use wireless or USB type-C connectivity for the Side Car. With

Side Car, you can Mirror or extend your display with an ipad or a MacBook. You can also use your iPad on your Mac as an input tool with the Apple Pencil using the Side Car feature.

Bug Fixes in iPADOS 13.4 beta version

There are a lot of bud fixes with the iPadOS 13.4. First, they fixed the camera viewfinder showing just a black display. They also addressed some issues in photos showing it using excessive storage. Apple has also resolved some issues with photos that may prevent sharing an image to messages if you have iMessaging disabled. Another problem fixed is in the mail app where messages in mail appear out of order and the conversation list may display empty rows, mail crashing when tapping the 'Share' button in 'Quick Look.' Also fixed is the issue with cellular data showing

'OFF' even when it is turned ON in Settings. Safari also had a bug fixed where webpages may not be inverted whenever 'Dark mode' and 'smart invert' are enabled at the same time. Also fixed on Safari is the issue of CAPTCHA not displaying correctly on some webpages.

For iCloud, they fixed the bug where iCloud Drive appears to be available in Apps even when users are not signed in to iCloud.

Apple went ahead to fix a bug within Apple music where music videos don't stream in high quality. They have also fixed an issue with shortcuts option not appearing correctly when sharing a screenshot.

Accessories for the iPad Pro and How they Function

Whether you got the bigger 12.9" or the regular 11" iPad Pro, the accessories listed in this section are compatible.

Apple Pencil 2

This is one accessory you should get alongside the iPad Pro. Apple Pencil 2 is a great tool to have even if you are not an artist. You can use it to navigate your iPad easily and it also serves as an extension to your fingers.

Magic Keyboard

The Magic Keyboard connects wirelessly to the iPad Pro. It has a unique hinge that keeps the iPad Pro floating in the air. The magic keyboard comes with backlit keys and a trackpad integrated into the keyboard, which supports multi-touch gestures. The keyboard also features pass-through charging on the additional USB-C port that comes on it—this free up your iPad's USB-C port for other uses. The Magic keyboard comes for $300 for that of the 11" iPad Pro and $350 for the 12.9" iPad Pro

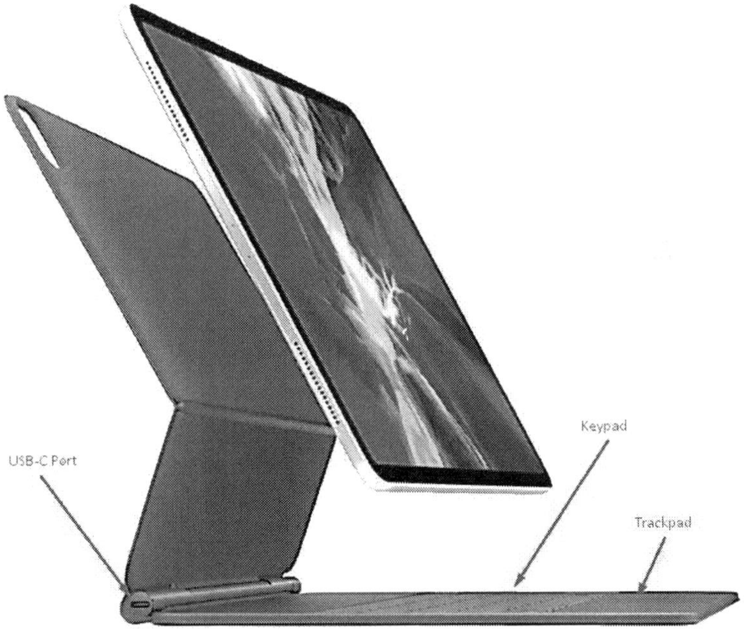

Magic Trackpad 2

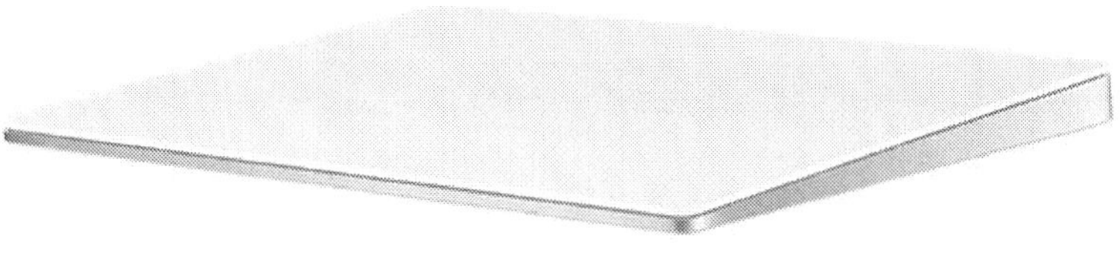

The magic trackpad is a standalone device that gives users more control and gesture ability on any iPad Pro running on iPadOS 13.4. Some users prefer the magic trackpad over the magic mouse because it provides more stability and response to gestures and moving around the operating system.

How to Check Mouse or trackpad battery life

You can easily track your mouse or trackpad battery life right from the home screen using the battery widget. Swipe from left to right on the home screen to reveal the battery widget. Under "Batteries," you will find your iPad, magic mouse, and trackpad's battery life.

Trackpad Pointer Customization

You can customize your pointer experience on the iPad Pro. To do this, go to 'Settings' > 'Accessibility' > Under 'Pointer Control', you can animate your pointer and allow it to adapt to elements on the screen by toggling ON the 'Pointer Animation.' You can also enable the pointer to continue moving after you lift your finger from the trackpad by enabling 'Trackpad Inertia.' Another pointer customization you can carryout is the scrolling speed. Users can either increase or decrease the scroll speed of the pointer. You could also hide the pointer and change pointer size and color under the 'Pointer Control' menu.

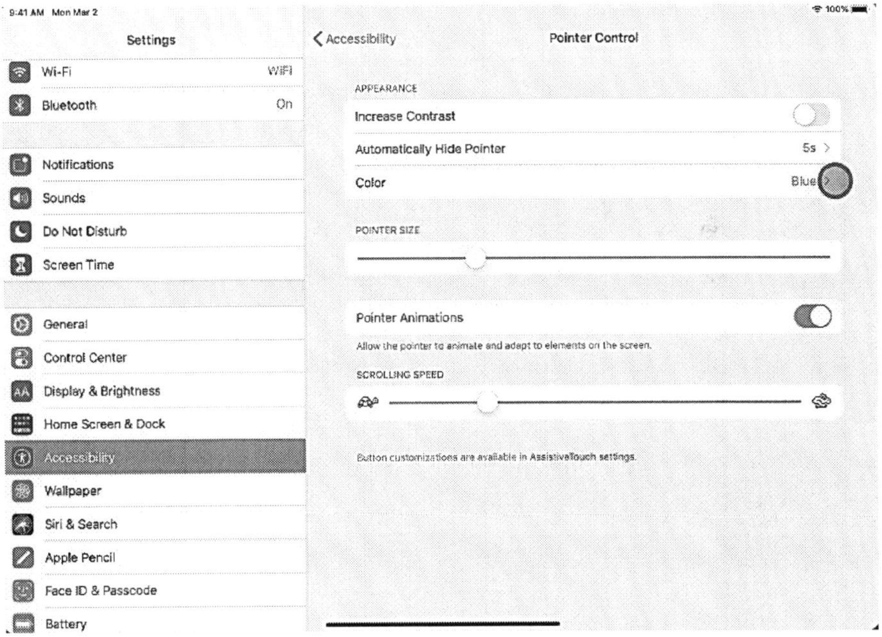

Magic Mouse and Trackpad Settings

You can customize your trackpad settings by simply going to 'Settings'> 'General'> 'Trackpad and Mouse.' Here you have the option to customize the trackpad speed, toggle ON or OFF the 'Tap to click,' 'Two Finger secondary click,' and 'Notification scrolling' options. The two-finger secondary click is another name for right-click. This opens up context menus or quick action shortcuts when an app icon is clicked with two fingers. Secondary click settings enable you to determine what part of the magic mouse should activate a secondary click action. The options include right, left, or Off. Turning Secondary click OFF means right-click or left-click on the mouse would not trigger a secondary action. Finally, it is ideal to enable the 'natural scrolling,' 'tapping to click' and 'two-finger secondary click' options.

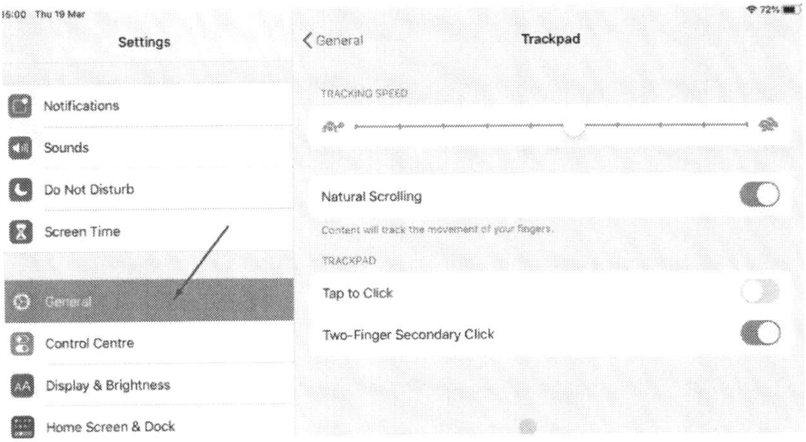

Scrolling through pages with the trackpad

On the trackpad, you use one finger to move the cursor around. But you need two fingers to scroll through a list or a webpage—swipe two fingers up to scroll down and two fingers down to scroll up.

Magic Mouse 2

There are two generations of the Magic Mouse, the first (Magic mouse 1) and the second generation (magic mouse 2). Magic mouse 2 is similar to the previous generation. It still has a multi-touch glossy surface along the top with physical right and left buttons. The big visual difference between the magic mouse 2 and the previous generation is at the back. There is no longer a removable panel for swapping batteries. Instead, it has an inbuilt battery and a lightning connector for charging the battery internally. The magic mouse delivers nine hours of use with two minutes of charge and two hours to get fully charged, which gives up to a month of use without having to recharge it.

Under the mouse is a switch which, when turned ON, allows the mouse to start pairing. There is no LED light on the mouse to know when it is ON or OFF, so you will look at the available Bluetooth devices on your iPad Pro to find out if it sees it or not.

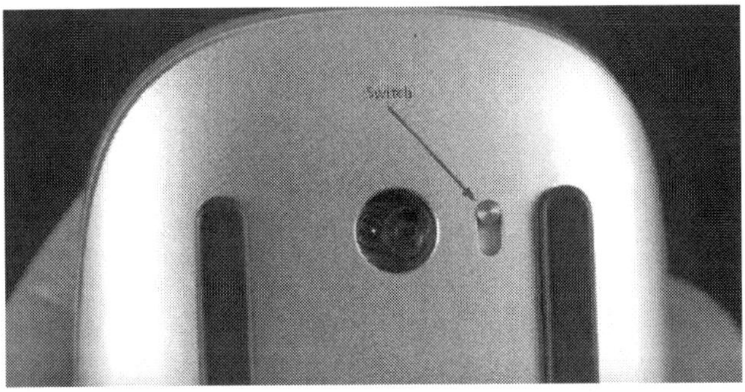

Scrolling Through Pages with the Magic Mouse

Scrolling through a list or website with the magic mouse is straight forward. To do this, while on a page, slide your finger on top of the mouse.

Moving the mouse pointer over an icon causes the icon to wiggle and zoomed in a bit with a shadow around it, but when the mouse cursor is placed over a button, it fades into the button. However, the mouse pointer changes to an I-beam pointer when placed in a search box or within a text area.

Dbrand Skin

Whether you are a case person or not, dbrand offers a bunch of different skins that can make your new iPad unique. They have tonnes of options and styles which provides scratch protection. This product can be found on the amazon web store

PaperLike

This is a screen protector that makes you feel like you are writing or drawing on a piece of paper. It gives the screen more grip when using the Apple pencil. It also gives users more control when writing or drawing due to the resistance it offers. It also reduces glare from the iPad Pro screen. The PaperLike is ideal for artists and illustrators.

Moko Smart Folio

This is an alternative to the Apple Smart keyboard folio. It looks and feels like othe official Apple folio, but it is four times cheaper than that of Apple.

Aer Tech Sling

This is a carrier bag for the 11 & 12.9 inches iPad Pro and can carry a bunch of other iPad accessories. There are tonnes of different slots for chargers, pencils and other iPad accessories.

Brydge Pro Keyboard

The Brydge keyboard makes your iPad Pro look like a Macbook. The Brydge keyboard has backlit keys with three different brightness levels which is an omission on Apple's Smart Keyboard folio. It is a full keyboard that also comes with some dedicated iOS buttons.

Brydge Pro Plus Keyboard

The Brydge Pro and Pro plus Keyboard are similar but for the addition of a trackpad on the Brydge Pro Plus iPad Pro keyboard.

Hyperdrive

This is the world's first dedicated USB-C hub for the 2018 and 2020 iPad Pro. It has the HDMI port, USB-A port, USB-C port with power delivery, SD slot, Micro SD slot and 3.5mm Headphone Jack. There are several colors of the Hyperdrive which matches the color (space grey or silver) of your iPad Pro as well as removable and replaceable translucent C-shaped grip made of soft materials that hold the hub in place without damaging the surface of your iPad.

Compass Pro

This is a brilliantly designed folding stand with three different angles for hands-free use from Twelve South. A big advantage of the compass pro over other iPad stands is that it takes up lesser space. The compass pro can be used at a lower angle which is perfect for drawing.

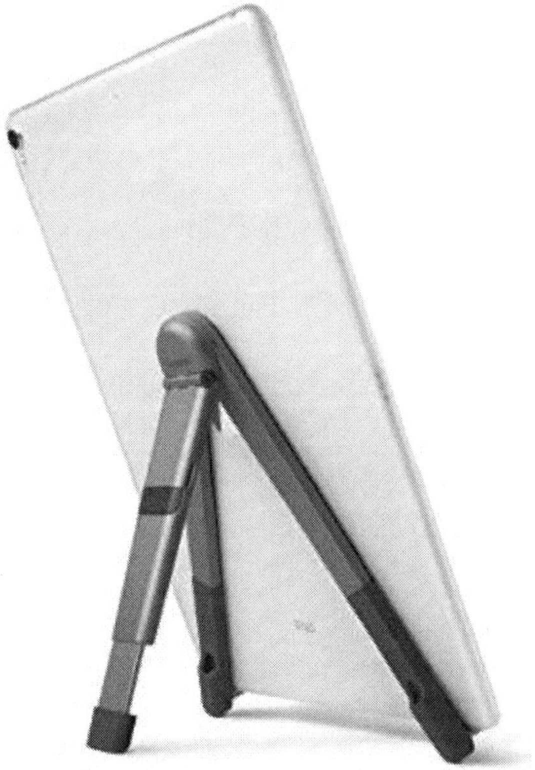

Airfly

This allows you to listen to your EarPod in places where it was hitherto impossible. E.g. the gym or on the airplane. The Airfly connects through a headphone jack and turns non-wireless audio sources wireless.

Connecting Harddrives to iPad Pro

With the new USB-C port on the iPad Pro, you can now connect a list of hardware devices.

GH5 & GH5X Cameras

The GH5, GH5x and other cameras with the USB-C port can be connected to the 4th Generation iPad Pro for seamless transfer of pictures between them. The steps to connect and transfer data between the iPad Pro and the GH5 are stated below;

- On the iPad Pro, open the Camera App
- Connect the USB-C cable to the Camera and the other end to the iPad Pro and turn the camera ON.
- At the screen on the back of the camera, a Menu will come up with the message "PC search", tap on it.
- When the "PC Search" is activated, all the videos and images on the GH5 or GH5x are displayed on the iPad. Tap on the images you wish to move to the iPad memory and click on "import". You can also edit the videos or images on the iPad

with several iPad video and picture editing Apps that can be installed.

GoPro 7

Footages captured by drones can be accessed on your iPad Pro. You can connect the iPad Pro directly to the USB-C port of the drone or attach it to the GoPro 7. If you are connecting it directly to the Drone, ensure the drone is powered OFF, before attaching the USB-C cable to the iPad Pro and the Drone. If the connection is made while the drone is powered ON, the media transfer will not be activated; it would only charge your iPad. After plugging and powering ON the drone, wait for it to initialize then the file transfer mode is activated automatically. Select the files you want and click on "Import" to move them into the iPad storage. Alternatively, the drones SD card can be used together with a Netbox 2.0 to transfer the images or video footages captured by the drone.

Plug in a USB-C cable straight into the side of the GoPro, then plug the other end into your iPad Pro to access all the images and video footages from the GoPro on your iPad Pro.

NetBox

Data can be transferred seamlessly from the iPad pro to an SD card using netbox. Install a Netbox App on your iPad Pro. Insert an SD card into the netbox which is then wirelessly connected to the iPad Pro. Using netbox to transfer data from an iPad Pro to an SD card eliminates the need to attach a card reader to the iPad Pro using a USB-C cable. This prevents the SD card reader from dangling by the side of the iPad while also maintaining a stable wireless data transfer.

After attaching the Netbox to the iPad Pro, go back to the netbox app on the iPad to have access to what is stored on the SD Card. You can transfer images and videos between SD cards inserted into the Netbox. (Note: Netbox comes with two USB-C ports). Tap on the Netbox App in the iPad Pro, you will find two hard drives connected. You can transfer from one SD card to the other or from the SD card to the iPad Pro.

Portable Console for gaming

These are Playstation and Xbox wireless consoles that are connected to the 4th Generation iPad pro via Bluetooth for enhanced gaming activities for those who prefer to use the iPad for mostly gaming activities.

To connect a wireless PS4 gamepad to the 2020 iPad Pro, Hold 'Share' and the 'PS' Buttons together at the same time until the light on the gamepad flashes. On the iPad Pro, go to 'Settings' > Bluetooth' > tap on the name of the gamepad on the list of devices to be paired to the iPad Pro.

External HDD Support

You can attach an external hard drive to the iPad, then drag and drop files to and from the external storage device. Connect an external Hard Disk to the iPad Pro using a USB-C cable.

Apple Pencil 2

The second generation Apple pencil was launched alongside the 2018 Apple iPad Pro. The Apple Pencil 2 only works with the 2018 and 2020 iPad Pro. The old pencil is not compatible with the 2020 iPad Pro due to the switch from Lightning port to the USB-C port. The second generation pencil has a new magnetic charging system that older iPads don't support. The pencil 2 looks and feels noticeably better in design when compared to the old one.

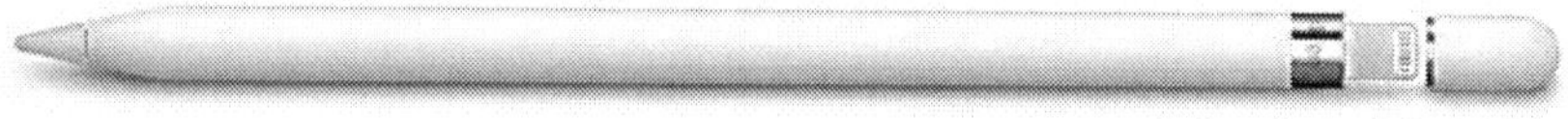

Old Apple pencil

Apple Pencil 2

The lightning connector and cap are no longer part of the second generation pencil, making it a bit shorter. It has a new mouth finish, thinner and has one flat side making the new pencil more comfortable in the hand. Unlike the original apple pencil, the new pencil tip does not wear out and doesn't come with a extra tip.

To pair the apple pencil 2 to the 2020 iPad Pro, place it by the side of the iPad pro where we have the pencil connector and it will magnetically snap into place; a prompt will come up on the screen requesting you to connect the pencil for wireless charging.

Any time the pencil is attached to the iPad Pro, its battery life is displayed. The battery life of the pencil can also be seen on the battery widget on the widget page. The great thing about this method of charging is that the magnetic connection is secure. There is less concern about losing the pencil while carrying the iPad around. There are also no issues with the iPad Pro case interfering with the pencil because every iPad Pro case features a cutout that allows the pencil to pair and charge without having to remove the case.

One of the few changes in the second generation Apple pencil is the new double tap feature. Double tap anywhere near the front end of the pencil and it switches to and from the eraser tool, making it quick and efficient to fix mistakes.

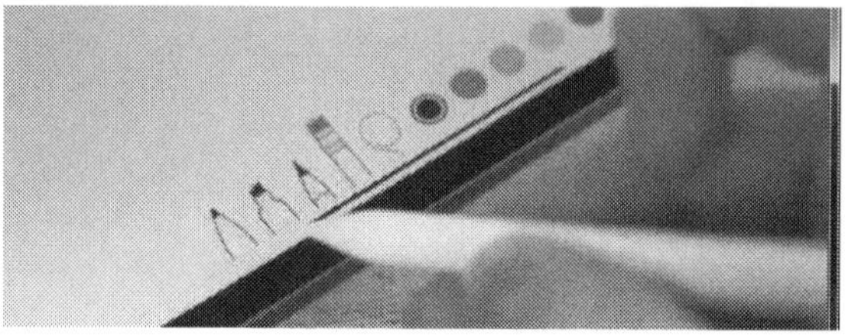

You can set "double tap" to do a few different things from the "Settings Menu" You can double tap to switch between a current tool and an eraser, switch between an existing tool and the last used tool, show color pallets or disable the double tap feature altogether. If you want to adjust the double tap durations

- Go to "Settings
- Tap on "Apple Pencil"

There are a few third-party apps that support the double tap feature including

- Procreate
- Concepts
- Liquid text
- Omnigraffle 3 etc

Charging the Apple Pencil 2 for a few seconds when the battery gets low give some minutes of use. You can purchase the 2nd Generation Apple Pencil on Apple's website for $129.00 and you can even get it engraved for free.

What the Apple Pencil Can Do?

- You can use it to navigate anywhere on the iPad Pro.
- It brings out spotlight search by swiping down from the center of the screen
- You can use it to type and also activate the iPad Pro Keyboard flipping feature.
- It is used for gestures like swiping up on the Home bar to go Home, accessing the control bar or long pressing to simulate a forced touch.
- The Apple Pencil detects pressure and tilts giving users a feel just like using an actual pencil, pen or marker.

- The "palm rejection" feature allows users to rest their palm on the screen while drawing.
- Documents and contracts can easily be signed using the Apple Pencil.
- With the AI machine learning on the iPad Pro, iPadOS 13.4 is smart enough to understand and read handwritten text allowing you to find words using spotlight search.

Pairing the Apple Pencil 2

After setup is complete, the next step you need to take is to pair the Apple Pencil to your device.

- Take the Apple Pencil OFF the magnetic port and place it back on.
- It hops in and a dialogue box pops up on the screen instructing you to pair the pencil. Click on "Connect"

- A "Welcome to Apple Pencil" dialogue box pops up on the screen. Click on "Continue" to navigate to the next setup screen. A tutorial on how to explore the Double Tap feature of the pencil is presented. Click on "Done" to complete the Apple Pencil pairing process.
- Take the Pencil OFF and put it back ON to charge it. The percentage of charge is displayed on the screen as soon as you replace the pencil on the magnetic port.

Smart Keyboard Folio

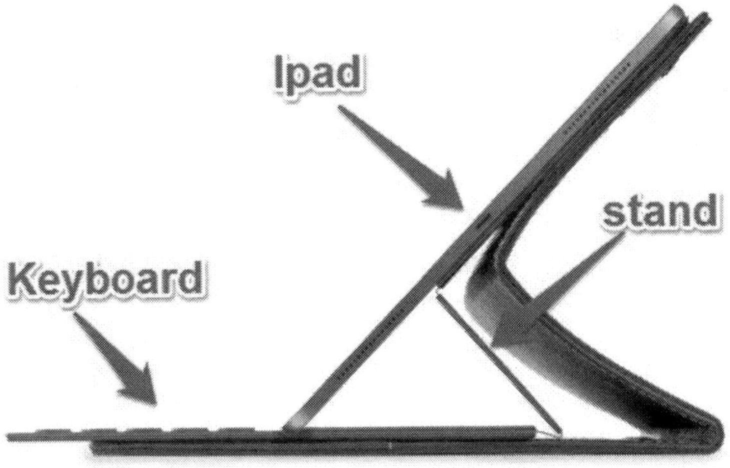

The smart keyboard folio is a full-sized keyboard that offers front and back protection for the iPad Pro. It connects to the smart connector at the back of the iPad using magnets. The keys on the smart keyboard folio are the same butterfly keys found on the MacBook, MacBook Air and MacBook Pro. The whole keyboard is covered in a solid piece of plastic light material making it spill and dust resistant. The smart keyboard has two viewing angles that lock the iPad well into place, which is excellent for watching movies or typing on a desk. The smart keyboard folio is easy to get off the iPad Pro and the keys are not active when the folio is fully opened up with the keyboard flap resting at the back of the iPad.

Smart Folio Lock and Unlock

The iPad Pro can be set to lock itself when the smart folio is closed and unlock itself when the smart folio is open. To set this up, go to 'Settings' > 'Display & Brightness' > scroll down and ENABLE 'Lock/Unlock.'

Chapter 3

Setting Up the iPad Pro

You can set up your iPad Pro as a New iPad or restore information backed up on your iCloud account from previous iPad or iPhone. The step by step setup process are listed below:

- Press and Hold the Power button at the top of the iPad until the Apple logo appears on the screen.
- Swipe up from the bottom of the screen to reveal the language options. Select your Language and swipe to the left to select your country or region.

- If you have the iPhone or iPad running iOS 11 or later, you can use the "Quick Start" option.
- Connect the old iPad or iPhone to the New iPad Pro.
- Hold the camera of the old iPad or iPhone over the iPad Pro to scan the circle displa-yed on the iPad Pro Screen.
- First on the setup page is "Data and Privacy". Set up the Data and Privacy and tap "Continue"
- Next, setup Face ID. The Face ID is an improved security feature on iPhones and iPads. Click on "Continue" to access the Face ID camera. Move your face around the camera to get all part of your face captured and click Continue when Face ID is setup.
- "Apps & Data" is the next item in setup process. You are asked to either restore

from your iCloud backup or from your iTunes backup or set up as New iPad or move Data from Android. If you have iPad or iPhone data backed up on your iCloud or iTunes account, you can transfer them to your new iPad Pro. You could also move data from an Android device into your device. Tap on "Continue" to move to the next step.

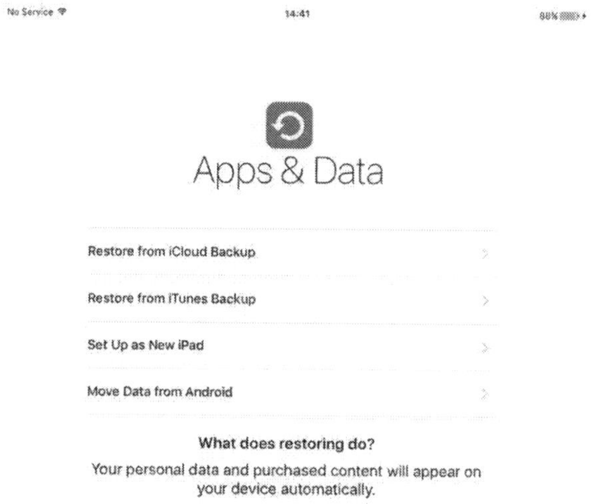

- Pay is next. Set up Apple Pay to enable you to add a debit or credit card to your Apple wallet to make seamless purchases on the Apple stores or any other stores.

You can skip this step during set up and do it directly in the wallet later. Click on "Continue"

- Next is on set up menu is Siri, go ahead and set it up or do you can do that later.

- Next to the Siri Setup is the App Analytics. App Analytics allows you to share data with Apple about your iPad Pro's performance. Tap on the "Share with Apple" otherwise, click on "Don't share" to protect your privacy. Click on "Continue"

- True Tone Display: The "true tone display" when enabled adjusts the color temperature of the iPad screen in relation to the prevailing amount of light in that environment. You can see how the screen displays with or without true tone by clicking on the button "See without True Tone Display."

You can setup true tone going to 'Settings' > 'Display and brightness' > 'True Tone'

- Finally, click on "Continue" to start the restoration process from iCloud. This could take a little while.
- When restore is complete, swipe up to unlock the screen and key in your pass-code.

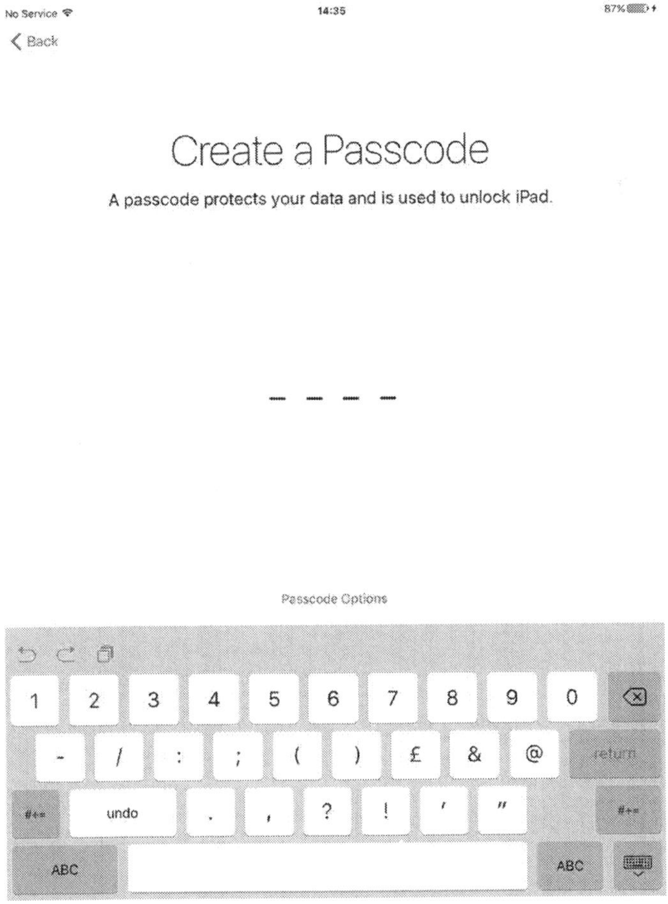

- Click on "Continue" and it takes a moment to set up your Apple ID. A brief guide on how to use features of the iPad like Screen Time, navigation gestures, Siri Commands, pops up on the screen in slides. Click on "Continue" to go through this guide until you arrive at the "Welcome to your iPad" Screen.

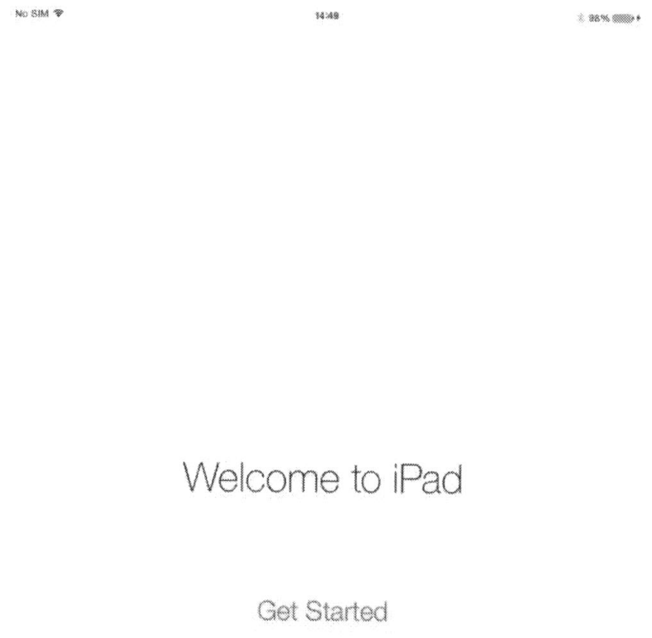

The 2020 iPad Pro Home Screen

The 4th Generation iPad Pro Home Screen consist of Apps icons at the right, "Today View" with Widgets on the left, and an Apps Dock at the bottom.

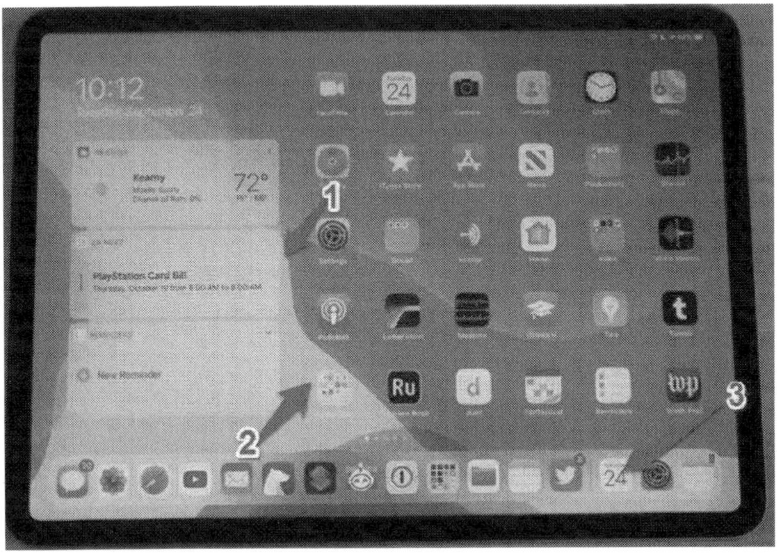

1 - Today View with Widgets

2 - App icons

3 - Apps Dock

Gestures Controls

Gestures, trackpad and mouse controls are the way to navigate, multitask, access various features and apps on the iPad Pro. The iPad Pro is the very first iPad without a "Home button" making it essential for users to learn how to navigate around it using gestures and clicks.

In this section, we will look at on-screen gestures, magic trackpad gestures and magic mouse gesture and their resulting effect on the iPad.

On-Screen Gestures for iPad Pro

Switching Apps & Going Home

Two unique gestures that the iPad has always had are the five fingers to close apps and four fingers to swipe between apps. With the five fingers to close, grab in a pinching motion with all five fingers spread across the app screen and with the four finger swipe you can switch between apps.

Access notification center

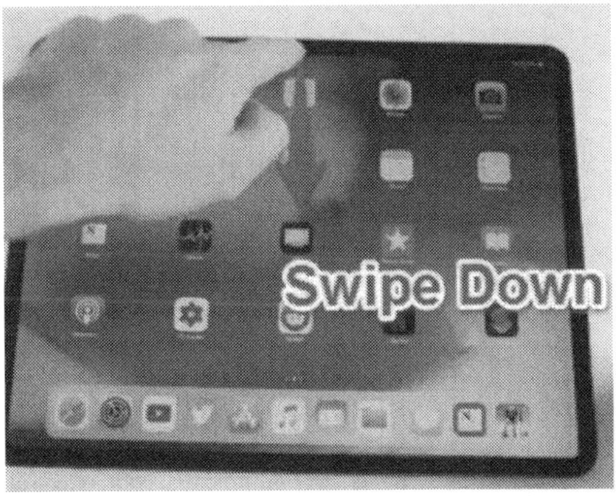

Swiping down from the top middle opens up the notification center. Here you will find any recent notifications you may have missed including notifications set to deliver quietly. Swipe up from the bottom edge to go back to the home screen.

Access the Control Center

To access the control center, swipe down from the top right of the screen.

You can adjust settings and other handy iPad features in the Control Center. To dismiss the control center, swipe up or tap anywhere on the screen outside the control center.

Swipe Bottom Up and Hold

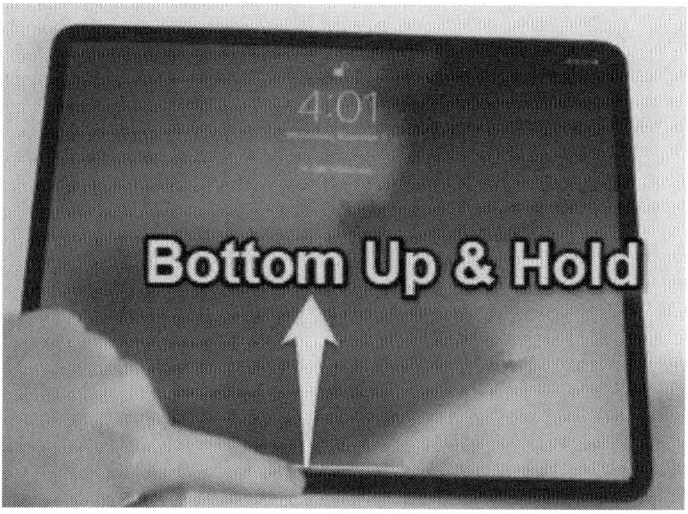

To unlock the iPad Pro, swipe up from the bottom of the screen then use Face ID or Password to authenticate. However, if you swipe from the bottom up and pause in the middle, the App Switcher mode will be activated. There you will find all opened Apps. The App Switcher can also be accessed by pinching-in with your four fingers at the center of the screen. You can also do this while in any application.

To open an app in the app switcher, tap on it. When you are done with an app, swipe up from the bottom edge of the App to go back to your home screen. Alternatively, you can go to the Home screen from an app by quickly pinching four or five fingers together.

View Recent Files in an App

To find recent files you worked on in an App, press and hold the app icon. This works with Keynote, Files, Pages, Numbers and more.

Force Close an App

You can force close an app while in the app switcher by swiping up on the app.

Add an App to the Dock

You can add an app to the dock any time you wish. Touch and hold the app, then drag it to the dock.

Swipe Left or Right

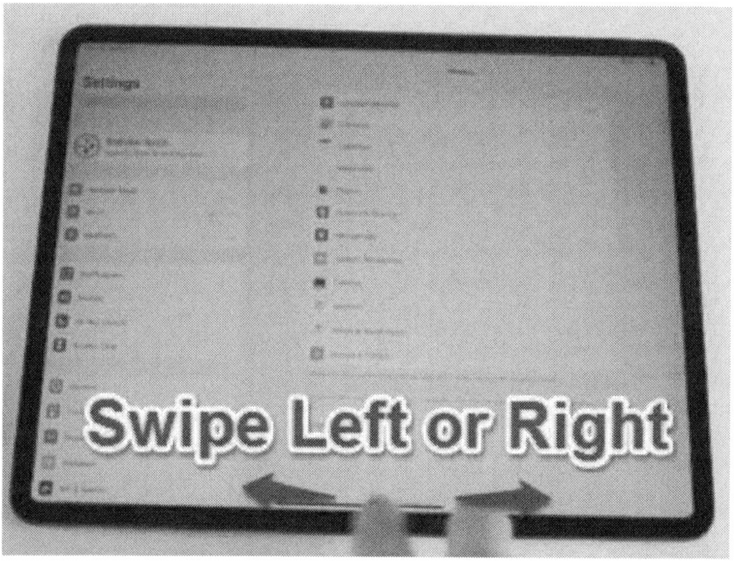

To get in andoout of applications quickly, you swipe on the bottom bar (Home bar). This is the most used gesture besides going to the Home Screen.

Swipe Dock Up

Apple upgraded the dock in the iPad Pro, so it does not just sit at the bottom of your Home Screen, you can pull it up within any app by swiping it up or swipe down to close it.

You can also switch sides of apps in the multitasking window. This is done by swiping on the grab handle at the top of the window and switch sides. You can switch back and forth to choose which app you want on the left and which one on the right. If you pull down the grab handle of an app in multitasking mode, it detaches the app and moves it into slide over mode. To slide over an app, swipe the grab handle to the side and when you need it again, you pull it back to the screen.

Put iPad Pro to Sleep

To put your iPad to sleep, press the sleep/wake button at the top. Tap the screen to wake it back up.

Access Spotlight search

You can search for Apps or anything on your iPad Pro with the aid of "spotlight search". Swipe down from the center of the Home screen to use Spotlight search and swipe up from the bottom edge to go home. Spotlight search allow you to search the entire iPad for apps, text messages, emails, etc.

Mouse and Trackpad Pointer Gestures

With the introduction of trackpad support in iPadOS 13.4, we will be looking at some handy tips to help you navigate your 2020 iPad Pro seamlessly in this section.

Going to back to Home screen Using Your Pointer

There are several ways to move directly to the home screen from any app on the iPad Pro. The first metho is to move the pointer down to the Home bar at the bottom of the screen. When you do so, you will realize the pointer snaps into the home bar, when this occurs, click on the mouse or tap on the trackpad if you are using a trackpad and it takes you to the Home Scr-een.

Another method to move to the home screen is with the four-finger swipe-up gesture on your trackpad. Also, you can get to the home screen by carrying out a long one finger swipe down on the trackpad as if you are trying to scroll past the home bar. If you are using the magic mouse, left-click and perform a long drag down of the mouse pointer, and it will take you to the home screen. A fourth method of doing this is to carry out a four-finger pinch-out gesture on the trackpad.

How to reveal the App Switcher using Trackpad

You can reveal the app switcher using the iPad Pro Trackpad. To do this, on the trackpad, swipe up, hold, then release, using four fingers. Another method of revealing the app switcher using the trackpad is to swipe down pass the home bar with one finger, hold, then release. You can also do this with the mouse, however, instead of swiping down, left-click on the home indicator and drag it up, then release.

How to Reveal the Dock Using Trackpad or Mouse

To reveal the dock, move your pointer down to the bottom of the interface, and the dock pops up.

How to Reveal the Notification Center Using Trackpad or Mouse

To reveal the notification center, move your cursor up to the upper left corner right by the date and time. The pointer will snap into the date and time, and then you click. Once your pointer locks on to the date and time, click to reveal the notification center. Another way to open up the notification center is to drag up pointer as if you want to drag past the top of the display. You also do this even when an app is open, and the notification center will be revealed.

How to Reveal Control Center Using Trackpad or Mouse

Trackpad and mouse gestures to reveal the control center and notification center are similar. Simply move the pointer to the upper right-hand corner, when it snaps into place with the battery and network icon, tap on the trackpad. This will reveal the Control Center. Alternatively, move your pointer pass the top of the upper right corner and this, too, will open the control center interface.

How to Expand the Control Center Elements with the Pointer

To expand the various control center elements, click and hold on the item. You can also press the control key on the paired keyboard and then click on a control center element to initiate an alternate click. Alternatively, you can use a two-finger tap on the trackpad while the cursor is on the control center element to expand it.

Revealing Widget on the Home Screen with a Mouse or Trackpad

You can open 'today's view' on the home screen using a single finger swipe to the right on the magic mouse. You can do the same on the trackpad using two-finger swipe to the right to open 'today's view,' and two-fingers swipe to the left to hide it.

How to Open Spotlight Search

You can reveal spotlight search from your trackpad using a two-finger swipe down and swipe up with two-fingers gesture to hide spotlight search. You can do the same on the magic mouse, but you need one finger swipe down to reveal Spotlight search, and one finger swipe up to hide it.

Revealing Context Menus

When you tap and hold on an icon using the trackpad, it simulates a long press which reveals the context menu. If you press the Ctrl key on your keyboard and simply tap on an icon, it initiates an alternate click and also shows your quick action shortcut menus for that icon. A two-finger tap on an icon simulates a mouse right-click, which also is a quick and easy way to reveal the context menus of any app.

How to move Home Screen App Icons with the Aid of a Trackpad or Mouse

Moving apps around on the home screen in ipadOS 13.4 is straightforward. Simply click and drag the app icon to where ever you want it to be. The method is the same for trackpad and mouse.

Using Pinch Gesture on the Trackpad to zoom

You can use the pinch to zoom gesture on the trackpad for apps like Safari and maps. Pinch-out to zoom in, move around the interface with two fingers and pinch-in to zoom out. You can also swipe between pages in Safari using two fingers back or forward gestures. This is also applicable to the magic mouse, except that you need a single finger in this instance to swipe back and forth.

Swiping Between Apps

To swipe between apps, first, open up the app > do a three or four finger left or right swipe on the trackpad to swipe between each of your opened apps.

How to use Split View

Engaging a split-screen with the pointer is as easy as doing so using on-screen finger gestures. All you do is click and drag one of the applications you want to add to your split view to the left or right side of an existing application. You can manipulate the space as desired, and you can change the aspect ratio of the opened apps by dragging the borderline in the middle. You can also engage slide over for apps. To do this, drag an app from the dock and drop it right in the middle of the split view demarcation. You can add as many apps in the slide over stack by dragging them to the split-screen demarcator. To switch between slide over apps within the stack, use a three-finger swipe on the stacked apps from your trackpad. If you swipe up with three-fingers, all the apps within your stack will be revealed. Finally, you can close individual apps within the stack by swiping up on the trackpad.

How to hide/show apps added to Slideover Stack

With the pointer input, you can easily hide or show your slide over apps by simply using the pointer to push it to the right edge.

Text Ediitng with the Trackpad or Mouse Pointer

Selecting individual word: With pointer control on the trackpad, you can easily select individual words by placing the I-beam cursor over the word and double-tap to select that word.

Selecting a block of text: You can highlight a block of text by placing the I-Beam cursor on a word within the range and triple-tap with a finger on the magic mouse or trackpad to select the entire block of text.

Selecting Specific items: You can select specific items using the click and drag or tap and drag option.

Moving Blocks of text around: You can move text or block of texts around easily by firstly, triple-tapping on the block of text, and then click and drag them to a new position.

Advanced Gestures

Working with multiple apps

You can activate multitasking by picking two apps with your fingers. Tap and hold on one app, then quickly tap on another app, move the first app to the side and this combines them in a split view. This also works with dock apps, pick an app in the dock, slide it all the way home while still holding it, tap another app and move it over to the side to open both apps side by side.

Improvement in Drag & Drop Movements

With iPadOS 13.4 powered iPad Pro you can pick up the item (e.g. Image) from one app (picture app), do a quick swipe home, open up the other app (e.g. Message app) while still holding the item and drop it in. You can also pick several items at the same time. Tap and hold the first item while using your other finger to swipe others towards it. This gesture holds several items as a unit and you can drop them in a separate app.

Selecting Text by Double Tapping

You can select entire text by double tapping on the onscreen keyboard with two fingers. Slide across the keyboard to drag the gesture points around the selected text.

Three fingers Copy and Paste

To copy a text on the iPad Pro, pinch-in using three-finger gestures and pinch-out to paste the text.

Three Fingers Undo and Redo

You can undo and redo actions on the iPad Pro by swiping right and left on the screen respectively with three fingers.

Apple upgraded the dock in the iPadOS 13.4, so it does not just sit at the bottom of your Home Screen, you can pull it up within any app by swiping it up or swipe down to close it.

You can switch positions of apps in the multi-tasking window. This is done by swiping on the grab handle at the top of each app window to switch sides. You can switch back and forth to choose which app you want on the left and which one on the right. If you pull down the grab handle of an app in multitasking mode, it detaches the app and moves it into slide over mode. To slide over an app, swipe the grab handle to the side and when you need it again, you pull it back to the screen.

Rearrange Apps

You can rearrange apps on the iPad's Home Screen by pressing and holding an app until the menu to "Rearrange Apps" pops up and this activates the wiggle effect on all the apps. You can now drag the apps to whatever position you want. You can as well drag an app to the Dock in this mode.

How to Pin Widgets to Today's View on the Home Screen

You can pin your favorite widget(s) to the home screen for easy access. To do this, swipe over from the left - tap "Edit" to access several widgets. Under "PINNED FAVORITES," there are spots with the inscription "Drag a Widget here to pin." From the list of widgets displayed, tap and drag any app(s) you want to that spot. Continue to drag the apps until you have a list of apps you want to appear on the Today View. Tap "Done" at the upper left corner when you are done.

Three Finger Gestures To Copy, Cut, Paste, Undo and Redo

You can copy text areas with a three-finger pinch-in gesture across the text. A Double pinch-in gesture on a text area cuts the text. A three-finger spread-out will paste a cut or copied text. A three-finger swipe to the left will undo an action while a three-finger swipe to the right redoes an action. Alternatively, tap on the text area with three-fingers to open the "Cut," "Copy," "Undo," "Redo," and "Paste" menu command.

How to Highlight or Select Text Area

You can select a word by double-tapping on the word. To select a sentence, triple-tap on the sentence. While to select an entire paragraph, quadruple-tap on the paragraph to selects everything.

Take a screenshot

To take a screenshot of your iPad Pro, press the power button and volume up button at the same time. Your screenshot will appear at the lower left corner of your device.

Alternatively, you can take a screen shoot with the Apple Pencil. To do this, swipe up from the bottom left corner of the screen with the pencil and it will take a screen shot. You can touch and hold the screenshot to share. Tap it to add annotations and text with markup, swipe left on the screenshot to dismiss it or search for it on your photos later.

Force Restarting the iPad Pro

If you ever need to "force restart" your iPad Pro, press and quickly release the volume up button, press and quickly release the volume down button and finally press and hold the top button until you see the Apple logo on the screen.

Face ID

Face ID is an enhanced security feature which identifies the face of the user before unlocking the phone. It provides secured access to app store, Apple pay, and authenticates user identity where ownership of the iPad Pro needs to be verified to prevent unwarranted access. To set up your password and change your Face ID

- Open Settings
- Tap Face ID & Passcode > enter the desired passcode > You would be taken to a window to pick apps that requires Face ID for access. E.g. iPad lock, Apple Pay, iTunes & App Store and Safari AutoFill etc.
- ENABLE apps or functions from the list of apps that you would need Face ID to access. If you don't intend to use Face ID to access any app or function turn all the options OFF. If you are going to use Face ID for some options, adjust their sliders accordingly.

Another feature that works with Face ID is the "Attention Aware Features". Click on the "Face ID and passcode" from the settings menu, scroll down a bit, Enable the "Attention Aware features." when the Attention Aware features is enabled, the iPad backlight won't go dim or turn OFF as long as you are looking at it. It senses that you are looking at the device and stays ON.

If you need to "Reset" Face ID for any reason, click on the "Reset Face ID" button and it will automatically go through the process of setting up Face ID.

For passcode, you can use number, words or a combination of both. Change a passcode by clicking on Change Passcode.

"Allow Access when locked" is a feature that allows you to set up apps and functions you can have access to when the iPad is locked. There is a list of them which includes - Today's view,

Recent notifications, Control Center, Siri, Reply with Message, Home Control, Return Missed Calls etc. You can Enable any of these functions to have access to them when the phone is locked.

Finally, you can setup Face ID for alternate appearance, in case you wear glasses or wig or anything that may alter your appearance.

Authenticating Face ID

When you make a purchase on iTunes or Apple store and Face ID is used to authenticate the purchase, to confirm the order, you need to double press the power/wake/sleep button for the purchase to go through.

Display Settings

True Tone can be enabled or disabled on the "display and brightness panel" in the "Settings" menu. You can also change "Auto lock" from

2 minutes to either 10 – 15 minutes or "Never". Display Zoom is also enabled or disabled in the Display setting. Display Zoom is better for people with bad sights.

Dark Mode

You can switch between light mode and dark mode on your iPad Pro. To switch to dark mode, go to 'Settings'> 'Display & Brightness'> under 'appearance,' select between light mode and Dark Mode.

You can set it to switch between light and dark mode automatically. This way, dark mode is activated when the sun goes down, and light mode is activated when the sun comes up. You could also set it to custom schedule to switch between dark and light mode.

Organize the Home Screen and The Dock

You can move apps around the Home screen by pressing and holding on the app you wish to move. You can also move it from the Home Screen to the dock. A lot of applications can fit into the iPad Pro dock. Multiple Apps can be moved around by simply pressing and holding an app, and then tap the other apps you intend to move alongside the main app. You can create a folder on the Home Screen by pressing and dragging apps on top of each another. Swiping from the bottom up while you are in an application pulls up the dock. This way you can open apps in the dock without having to go to the Home Screen.

You can change the layout of your home screen to accommodate more apps or make the app icons bigger. If you want more apps to fit into the home screen, go to 'Settings' > 'Home screen and Dock' > select 'More.' However, if you prefer the app icons to be bigger on the home screen, select 'Bigger.'

Customize the Control Center

Swipe down at the top right on your home screen to open the iPad Pro Control Center. The Control Center has different quick settings.

iPad Pro Control Center

Airplane mode

Airplane mode allows you to turn OFF cellular, Wi-Fi and Bluetooth when you are in an airplane to prevent radio interference.

Cellular

This allows cellular service to be turned ON/OFF. Turning OFF cellular fuction prevents iPad from accessing your mobile service provider.

Bluetooth

Bluetooth connectivity allows you to connect your phone to an AirPod as well as connect to other Bluetooth devices. AirDrop also uses Bluetooth connectivity to share files between Apple devices.

Wi-Fi

Allows you to turn ON/OFF Wi-fi connectivity. You can as well connect to a wifi network from the control panel.

Easy Access Control Panel

This is a little control panel that displays the current app using radio functionality. For instance, if you are listening to music or watching a youtube video, this panel gives you control of the media playing without having to leave the control center.

Lock Rotation

When the iPad is tilted horizontally, the screen display automatically changes its orientation to landscape. This returns to Portrait orientation when the ipad is rotated to a vertical position. Activating the "rotation lock" locks the phone to portrait orientation irrespective of whether the ipad is tilted horizontally or vertically.

Do not Disturb

The "Do not disturb" setting deactivates both visual and sound notifications from calls, text messages and other alerts. This is very useful when you are in a meeting, driving, or in a place where you don't want to be distracted. The "Do Not Disturb While Driving" is also a great control feature. When this is enabled, it will automatically send a text message to anyone who calls, notifying them you are driving and would respond to their call whenever you get to your destination.

Brightness Settings

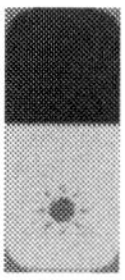

This allows you to increase or decrease the screen brightness. A haptic touch (force press) on the brightness icon gives you an option to turn ON/OFF "True Tone" and "Night Shift". True Tone takes the background lighting around you and adapts the iPad's screen to that automatically. Night Shift changes the tone of the screen depending on how well the room is lit in order to prevent glares from getting into your eyes. It also gets rid of some of the blue lights at the background to help your eyes adjust to the rays from the screen at night. This helps to protect your eyes. The night shift option can be schedule.

Volume Settings

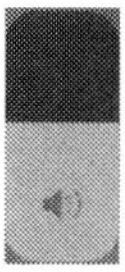

The volume icon is used to increase/decrease the iPad's volume.

Screen Mirroring

This allows you to mirror the screen of your iPad on another device such as a laptop, projector, Television etc.

Low Power Mode

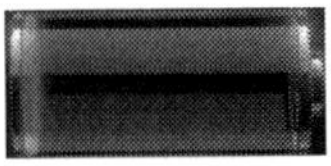

Low Power Mode when enabled saves the battery life of your iPad by getting rid of some minor features that takes up batteries power. Other optional controls that can be added to the control center are the timer, Flash light, Camera etc.

To customize the control center, go to 'Settings' › tap on 'Control Center' › 'Customize Controls.' At the top, we have a list of control icons in the control center, and at the bottom is a list of control icons you can add to the control center. This way, you can add and remove items from the control center. To remove an existing item from the control center, tap on the red button with a minus sign and to add an item to the control center, tap on the green button with a plus sign by the side of the item.

How to Use the Measure App

With LiDAR Sensor, the measure app in iPadOS 13.4 got a major boost in terms of accuracy and precision. To use the measure app, follow the steps below:

- Open the measure app to get started. 
- An instructions will appear on your screen, telling you to move your iPad around for the app to do a quick scan of objects around you.
- Move your iPad around until a circle appears on the scree. Move your device to get to the starting point of what you

intend to measure in the middle of your screen.

- Then tap the plus "+" sign at the bottom to add a point. If you make a mistake, tap the undo button at the top left corner to try again.
- Move your iPad so that the end point of the object you are measuring appears on your screen.
- Tap the plus "+" sign again to mark the end of your measurement. You can create multiple line measurements at the same time if you measure the dimension of an object.
- Tap the measurement to see different conversions to other units of measurement.
- Tap "Clear" at the top right corner of your screen to clear all measurement or start over.

- The app can automatically detect rectangles. If you move the camera over a rectangle, you will see an orange outline appear around it.

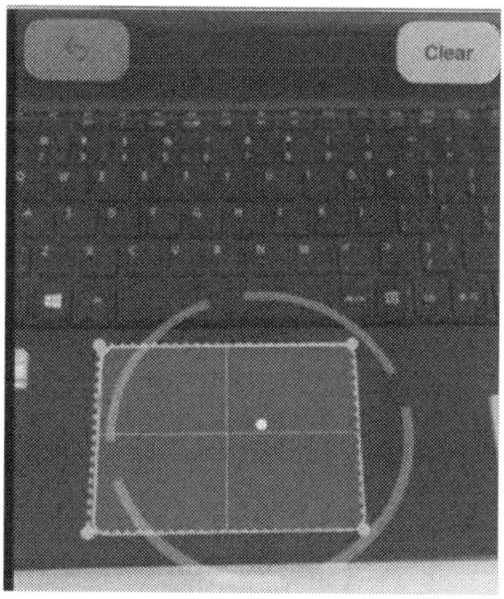

Tap the middle of the outline to quickly get the length and width of the rectangle at the same time.

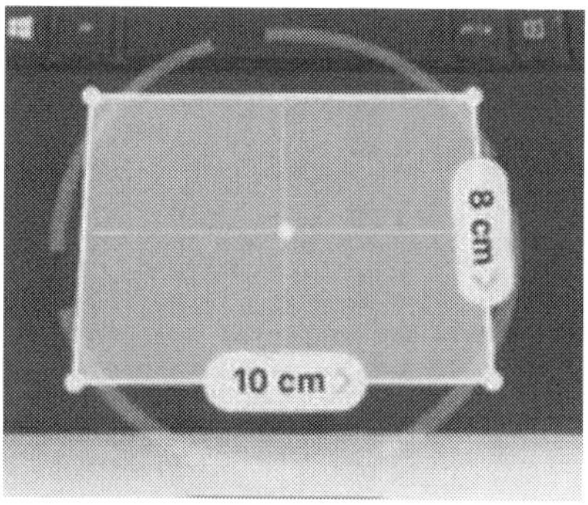

- Besides measuring length, you can use this app as a balancing tool. Tap "Level" at the bottom of the screen to switch to level mode. You can use this feature with your device vertically or horizontally.

- Set your iPad on a surface, you intend to get leveled. For instance a picture frame or a shelf.
- When you tilt the iPad, it tells you how many degrees you are from been leveled. When it is level, your screen will read 0° and the background will turn from black to green.

How to create Secure notes

- Launch the "Note Application"
- Create a New note.
- Tap on the upload icon  close to "done" and at the bottom, you will see several options including "Lock Note."
- Tap on "Lock Note". You will be requested to scan your face if you have the Face ID

enabled or you can put in your passcode and the lock would be added. You would need to unlock the note using either Face ID or passcode to view the content.

How to set up two-factor authentication

This is a security measure for iCloud services that request for two things instead of a single password to log into an online service.

Typically, the two-factors are usually a password and a code that the server sends to you via your cell phone. Requesting for two-factors instead of one makes it harder for the bad guys to pretend to be you. The following steps enable you to set it up via iCloud.

- Sign into your iCloud account
- Click on your username at the upper right-hand corner and from the drop-down, click on "Account Settings."

- Click on your Apple ID and this would launch a new tab on the Apple ID page. Click on "Manage your Apple ID"
- You would be required to sign in again.
- Click on "Passwords and Security." At this point, you will have to answer some security questions and click on "Continue". You would be taken to a 3 step notification screen on the risks of two-factor authentication.
- Next, click on "Add a phone number." This is the phone number through which Apple will send authentication codes. Ideally, it should be your iPhone or any phone that you would always have with you.
- Click on "Next." This introduces a window that asks for your four-digit verification code sent to the phone number you added. Click on "Verify"

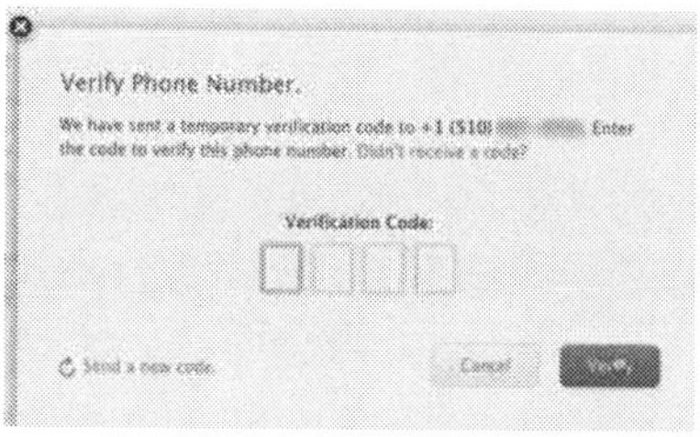

- Add an iPad or phone or both to the list of verification devices. What this does amongst other things is it allows Apple to send verification code by push notification instead of just SMS. Once again you will get a verification code sent to your phone, enter it in the space provided and click on "Verify".
- Get the "Recovery Key" that is displayed on the screen. The Recovery Key isanother code you can use to unlock your iCloud account if you don't have your phone with you. You will be able to log in with this verification key and your password. It is always adviced that your print out the recovery key and keep it in a secure place.

- Click "Done" to activate two-step verification and whenever you log into iCloud.com to manage your account or make purchase from a new device, get Apple ID-related support or use one of Apples web apps on iCloud.com, Apple will check to ensure you are who you say you are by sending a verification code to the phone your registered plus your usual password to get in.

Airdrop

Airdrop is an ad-hoc network service that allows you to wirelessly transfer files over Bluetooth and wifi between iOS devices and Macs. It could be from an iPhone to an iPad or from an iPad to an iMac or verse versa. When using Airdrop between an iPad and an iPhone, you can send photos, videos, contacts Passbook Passes, Voice Memos, Map Locations, and everything else that appears on a share sheet. When using Airdrop between two Macs, you can share virtually any file. There is no file size or type restrictions.

- Place your iPad next to the iPhone. Enable Wi-fi and Bluetooth are turned ON on both devices in the control center.
- Tap AirDrop in the control center and set it to "Everyone" to share with everyone or "Contacts Only Mode" to share with only people in your contact. The same process goes for the iPhone.
- Go to the iPad and find a file you intend to send and tap on it (e.g, a document)
- Tap ellipsis (...) on the upper right and click on the share option to access the share sheet. Tap on the device you wish to send the file to in the share sheet and the file is automatically sent.

- If you are using AirDrop on your Mac for the first time, you may need to adjust the settings on your Mac. To do this;
- Open finder and choose AirDrop in the left-hand column. The settings are in blue where it says "Allow me to be discovered by". Click on the little down arrow at the end of the statement and you will be presented with similar options to what is on iOS. (No one, Contacts Only, Everyone).
  - With this setup, you can now send files between the mac and any other iOS device.
  - Right-click or Ctrl-Click on the file you want to AirDrop, scroll to "Share" and click on "AirDrop."
  - The AirDrop window that pops up may take time to populate. Once the person you want to send the file to pops up, simply click on them and the file is sent.

Apple mobile system is geared towards freeing users from the use of physical cash and cards. Apple Pay uses Near Field Communication (NFC) and a technology called Magnetic Secure Transmission to make payments when you tap your iPad or iPhone on a payment terminal. When the iPad is held to a terminal, it sends a signal that simulates the magnetic strip on a debit or credit card. Apple Pay has browser payment in Safari and several Apps. You will need to confirm payment with your fingerprint or Face ID to purchase Apps or pay for items online. "Apple Pay Cash" allows users to send money to friends through iMessage or Split-the-bill and only Apple users can send money to each other.

How to Add Card to Apple Pay

Mobile payment system uses a technology called tokenization to keep card details secure. Once you add your card to the App, it generates a virtual account number and your real card number is never given to the merchants. If your phone is stolen, Apple Pay allows you to wipe your account details remotely which will remove your virtual wallet along with it. Below are the steps to add a card to your Apple Pay Wallet

- Open wallet app

- Tap  icon
- Scan your Debit or Credit Card

- Follow bank instructions
- Done, you card is now added to the Wallet App and Credit/Debit card is ready for Apple Pay

How to Remove Used Pass

The Wallet App is one of the ways to integrate Applepay into your iPad. Apart from being the best way to pay for items on the iPad pro, it is also used to store different passes (e.g. links to hotels, boarding tickets for flight etc). These Passes however needs to be removed after use. To remove a used pass, follow the steps below.

- Open the wallet app
- Tap on your card and your passes is displayed at the bottom.
- Tap on the pass
- Tap on the "i" option at the bottom right.

- Scroll down and tap on "Remove Pass". This will automatically remove it from the app.

How to deactivate Annoying pop ups

Depending on the site you visited, you may be experiencing some pesky pops-ups (mostly ads claiming you have won a gift card).

These are malware that slips in like a virus when you visit a questionable website or download an app. To prevent it from escalating, close up the pop-ups as soon as they appear. Don't click on the close "x" button that is on the ad; it will take you to yet another ad. Simply close your browser by swiping it up, then clean your phone's history.

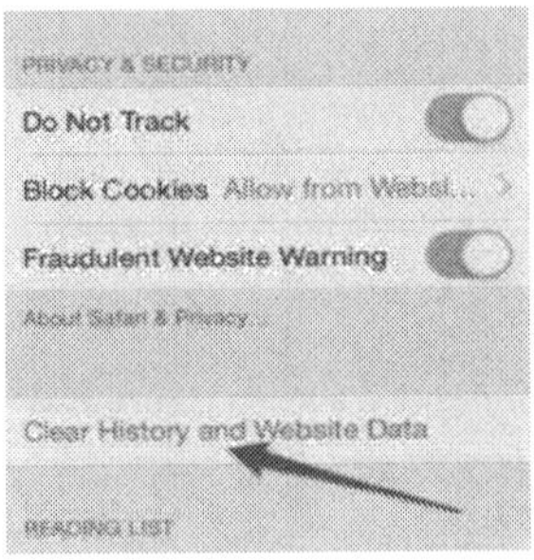

If the "clear History" doesn't work, carryout a full factory reset.

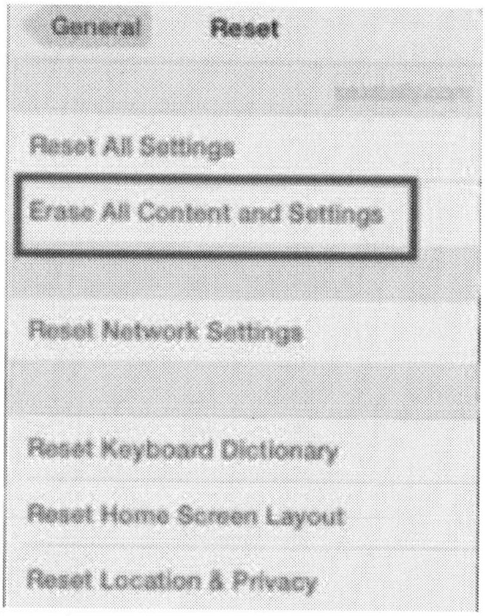

Before you do this, make sure your information is backed up to the cloud. Alternatively, you can install a Safari pop up blocker on your iPad. Finally, resist the urge to check out that free Amazon gift card you supposedly won.

Control Center Scan QR Code Shortcut

You can access control center QR code shortcut by:

- Going to settings

- Tap on Control Center
- Tap on "Customize Controls" Scroll up from the list and tap on "Scan QR Code" and QR Code shortcut will appear within the control center.
- Invoke the Control Center by going to the home screen
- Swipe down from the top right of the screen and you will find the Scan QR Code shortcut within the control center.
- Tap on it and it would take you to the camera app, this allows you to scan QR codes.

How to use Google Map on iCar app

The new iPadOS 13.4 allows you to listen to music, make phone calls, use a GPS app or install third-party map such as google map in your Car. Here are the steps to follow. This works on cars that have a smartphone interface

- Connect the USB-C adaptor from your car play system to your iPad.
- The carplay notification is displayed on the iPad when it is connected and the window is displayed on the car play system screen. This will work in any car that has the latest Apple carplay system updated to iOS 13.
- Using the control of the specific vehicle carplay, click on Google Maps. Google map displays traffic and other useful information

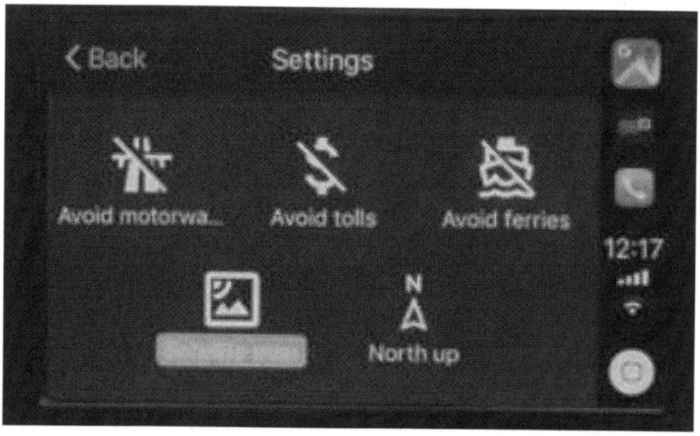

- Click on "Settings". Under the setting menu you have "Avoid Motorway", "Avoid tolls", "Avoid ferries", and "Satellite Map". Click on "Satellite Map."

- You can do a lot of things on the Google satellite map, for instance, adding a destination, zoom in to see where you are currently parked, etc.
- A quick "add destination" displays major places you could get direction to and from e.g, coffee shops, gas stations, restaurants, supermarkets, etc.
- Tapping on the coffee shop or gas station displays all the coffee shop or gas stations

options within your locality and the fastest routes to get there.

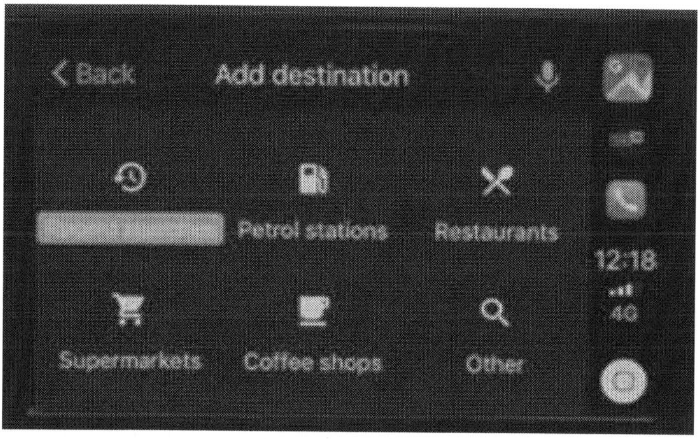

- Click on "Go" when you have selected your destination. As you drive along you will receive routing information.

How to Back up an old iPhone and restore it to iPad Pro

This will help you to retain all your contacts, text messages, applications, pictures, etc.

- Go to the settings of your old iPhone or iPad › click on your profile to access iCloud

- Tap on iCloud Backup. Make sure you have a recent backup. Click on "Backup" to have an up to date backup. This will take some time depending on the size of data to be backed up. After the backup process is complete, it will prompt you to Set up New iPad.
- While that is ongoing, carry out the initial set up process for your New iPad Pro and stop at the "Quick Start" window. Bring it close to the old iPhone to sign up automatically.
- On the old iPhone tap on "Continue." Then hold the old iPhone up to the camera to scan the little barcode displayed on the new iPad Pro. This will ensure everything is transferred over. You will be prompted to enter the passcode for the old iPhone on the New iPad Pro to set up the device. The backup information is then displayed

on the iPad pro. You would be prompted to either update backup before transfer or transfer without an update.

- Agree to the terms
- Tap on "Continue" to restore settings from your Backup and follow the set up prompts.

Chapter 4

Handy iPad Pro Apps

Notability

This is not a free App. It is a note taking App. You can take notes, highlight, erase, cut and move a section of text with a scissors, make sketches and voice record on the App with the Apple Pencil. Microsoft Outline is a free alternative to the Notability App.

Procreate

Procreate is an iPad app that lets you draw anytime anywhere with the world of art Media literally at your fingertips. Procreate is a powerful and intuitive painting and drawing app for the iPad.

Next

This is an App you can use to control smart thermostats, doorbells, cameras, etc in the home. You can control your thermostats, security for the home, and many more appliance from the iPad using the Next App.

Snapseed

Snapseed is a free App made by Google. It is a simple App to edit photos.

LiveX

LiveX controls Wi-Fi operated lights in the home. It allows you to switch ON or OFF lights, Change light colors and color temperature of Wi-Fi-controlled lights from the iPad. An altern-ative to this App is the Philip Hue App.

Filmic Pro

This is used for managing highend or more professional settings for the video function of the iPad Pro. If you are willing to get the most out of your iPad's video capabilities, then you need to download FiLMiC Pro for $15. It is packed with several features, which unlocks DSLR-like settings on your iPad Camera. FiLMiC Pro is one app that allows you to record videos from all four cameras at the same time. It gives you full manual control of your shutter speed, focus, frames per second, white balance, ISO, etc. You also get LOG V2 with the FiLMiC Pro, which, according to the developers, gives you up to 2.5 stops of additional dynamic range, which exceeds some DSLR cameras.

iMovie

This is a professional video editing App for the iPad Pro. You can add title, background music and Hollywood styled effects to your video clips.

Duolingo

This is an App that helps you learn new Languages.

LumaFusion

This is quite an expensive but powerful app. It is great for editing videos on the go. It has more features to the iMovie although a little bit complicated to use. You get all the short cuts you can use with this App by pressing the Command Key on the Smart Keyboard.

Udemy

Udemy is a platform where users upload their questions and get answers. You can do two things on Udemy, first create questions. Let say you know how to play the piano and you want to teach others how to play the piano, simply film yourself playing the piano and upload it to Udemy. They will pay you to take your course. The second thing you can do on Udemy is to take the courses.

Calendar

This allows you to add calendar events into your device. Just tap on a date or click on plus

"+" to add a new event, then pick the start time. This can also synchronize with Google Calendar in settings to ensure all events are available on the Calendar app.

Photos App

Photos app shows you all of the photographs you have taken with your iPad. To take a regular photo with your camera, press the big white shutter button at the bottom. Turn your iPad around for landscape photos. You can also use the volume up button to take pictures as well. There are several features at the top of the camera. You can turn ON or OFF the flash using the flash icon or keep it on "Auto". You can also turn ON/OFF HDR photos depending on the quality you are looking for, turn ON or OFF timer if you want to set it up for a selfie or put it on a stand. On the top right is the filter icon to add different filters to your photograph. Also, you can zoom in and out by pinching your fingers on the camera screen or press and hold the 1x zoom to bring up the zoom wheel. You can switch between the ultra-wide, and wide-angle lens by tapping on 0.5x, and 1, respectively.

To capture an image,

- Focus your camera on the image,
- Select the lens you want and
- tap on the shutter button or press the volume button

To change the focus point of your camera, tap on the position on the screen and the camera will focus on that point.

Taking Live Photos

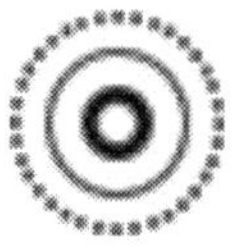

The live video functionality records videos before and after a picture you take. The general guideline is to keep live photos ON every time there is movement in the scene or whenever you are taking pictures of people. The live photo icon turns yellow when it is turned ON.

Flash

This is used in activating the camera flash if you wish to take flash photography. You have the option to turn it ON, OFF, or leave it at AUTO. However, the best recommendation in smartphone photography is to keep the flash OFF. This is because the flash on the iPad is relatively weak. It only works well when your subject is very close, and even then, you may end up with unnatural looking colors and other potential image quality problems. Because of this, it is better to leave the flash off, else get an external flash with a higher resolution like the Profoto C1 Plus Flash. But for most photography situations, even in low light, it is recommended that you keep the flash OFF.

Switching between Front Facing and Rear Facing Cameras

The 7 megapixels (f/2.2 Aperture) front-facing camera, also known as the selfie camera, shoots 1080 pixel videos at 120 frames per second. The front-facing camera is toggled ON by tapping the camera flip icon .

Other Camera Settings

There are other settings on the camera for quality photo shoot experience. E.g. time lapse (if you turn this ON, it would take a number of photos over a period of time which you can stitch together), portrait mode (it makes your photos come out better with different lighting effects i.e, studio lighting, contour lighting, stage lighting etc), Square (for Instagram), panoramic (takes several photos and stitch them together into one big panoramic photo). If you take a portrait mode photo, open it and click on "Edit" to change the aperture from f16 to f1.4. This changes the amount of blur that is shown in the photo. To take burst photos, press and hold the shutter button. Then pick the best picture from the burst mode.

Swipe across the camera screen to go to video mode. This enables you to record videos. Tap on the red circular button to start recording. To stop recording, tap on the red circular button again. There are several options to choose from while recording. For instance - slow motion video (this is great for sports). At the top right of your video recording screen, it says HD and 60. What this means is that youoare recording at 1080P which represents a High definition at 60 frames per second. The iPad camera is built to record up to 4k at 60 frames per second, but this is not set up by default. You have to go in and tweak the settings.

To do this:

- ✓ Go to Settings
- ✓ Scroll down and tap on "Camera" option
- ✓ Tap "Record Video". This will allow you to pick between the different modes listed. (720p at 30fps, 1080p at 30fps, 1080p at 60fps, 4k at 60fps etc). Note: 4K at 60fps is only available at High-Efficiency Mode. The reason is that high efficiency takes less space on your iPad. The higher the resolution and fps, the more storage space required. To activate the High-Efficiency Mode, tap on "Settings" > "Camera" > "Formats" > You will realize that the "Most Compatible" is enabled, this won't work for 4k at 60fps. Tap on "High Efficiency" to enable it.

Map App

The Map app acts as a GPS. All you have to do on the map application is to search for an address, click GO and the app will give you step by step direction to get there.

Alarm

You can set the alarm by going to the alarm app. Tap on Add Alarm to set up alarm time. You can have these alarms to repeat at specific periods. For instance, you can set the alarm to go off same time every weekday or every Tuesday. You can also change the sound of the alarm. Another option is to choose whether you want snooze to be an option or not. This is valuable now that Face ID is an option to un-lock your phone. You can select the option to use your face to snooze alarm. That way, you have to look straight at your iPad to turn the alarm OFF; no more reaching to the side of your bed with sleepy eyes and pressing any button to snooze the alarm. Using Face ID to snooze an alarm will ensure you are awake. In addition to this, we have Bedtime. It tracks when you go to bed, when you wake up, sets up alarm that will correspond with that. This setting ensures you are getting the right amount of sleep each night.

Weather App

This shows you the weather in your current location and the weather for the days ahead. There are several weather apps to choose from in the App Store.

News App

The news app will show you the latest trending stories. There are several news app to choose from in the App Store.

Home App

The Home app allows you to connect any smart light, locks, or any smart technology you have in your home.

Microsoft Excel

This is one app that will handle all your spreadsheet needs on the iPad Pro. It allows users to add charts, annotations, edit basic data, and formulas.

Note

This is an easy way to keep track of what is on your mind by jotting them down. You can also draw on your note and save them by clicking DONE.

Stocks

The stocks app allows you to track whatever stock you have invested in your stock portfolio.

Apple Wallet

Stores your credit card details so you can easily have access to it when you are tapping on one of those creditocard terminals.

Podcast App

This allows you to listen to your favorite podcasts.

Calculator App

The calculator app allows you to do simple calculations. If you turn your iPad to the side while using the calculator app, you will get a scientific calculator which aids you to do more complex calculations.

Keynote

This app is used for preparing slides for presentations in seminars or lectures. It functions just like the Microsoft Power Point.

Pages

This is a word processor app just like the Microsoft Word application.

Artificial Intelligence Apps

Several AR Apps can take advantage of the LiDAR Sensor on the 2020 iPad Pro. AR apps are becoming even more realistic with the addition of the LiDAR sensor on the iPad Pro. Realistic object occlusion in iPad Pro allows AR objects to pass in front of and behind real-world structures captured on these apps. Also, improved motion capture and people occlusion are more accurate than ever on the 2020 iPad Pro and developers will be able to create apps with more immersive experiences. In the App Store, the AR apps are categorized into 'Remodel with AR,' 'Learn with AR,' 'Shop with AR' in the App Store. To search for these apps, go to the 'App Store' > click on 'Apps' > scroll down to 'Top Categories,' on the right side click on 'See All' > Click on 'AR Apps' on the top left. This will take you to a page where you will see several AR applications that support the LiDAR sensor to choose from.

iScape

This is an AI App for landscaping. If you want to see how trees, shrubs, flowers and pavers will look in your yard, then the iScape app is what you need.

IKEA Place

IKEA place is another exciting Artificial Intelligence app. It helps users get the right furniture for their homes and offices and the right positions to place this furniture.

Downloading Apps from the App Store

To download additional apps into your iPad, Go directly into the App store on your iPad - you could either scroll through some suggested applications, check out the top free apps or purchase paid apps.

The Games Tab: This has all kinds of fun game apps you could download and install. Some are free while others are paid.

The App Tab: This has a list of useful iPad Pro apps you could download.

Top Free: This is another way to get the top or most downloaded free apps. Click See All to see the entire free app list. Top free apps is a good indication of apps you should download in your iPad.

Organizing Apps on the iPad

To organize apps on the iPad, press and hold an App until they go into wiggle mode with an "X" on them. To move them around, press and drag each app to a different location. You could also move apps in and out of your dock. The dock is at the bottom of the screen and can display four apps at a go. To remove an app from the dock, press and drag it out of the dock. Click and drag any app you want in the dock from the top down. Click DONE when you are done moving the apps around. You can also delete apps you don't need by getting into the wiggle mode and click on X at the top right corner of any app you want to remove, then click DONE at the top right corner of the screen to finalize your changes.

Insert Apps in a Folder

If you wish to insert several apps in a folder, activate the wiggle mode, then click and drag the app on top another app. This automatically creates a folder and adds the apps into the folder. You can also change the name of the newly created folder to whatever you wish. To pull out the app from the folder, click and drag it out.

Chapter 5

iPad Pro Settings

Battery Insight

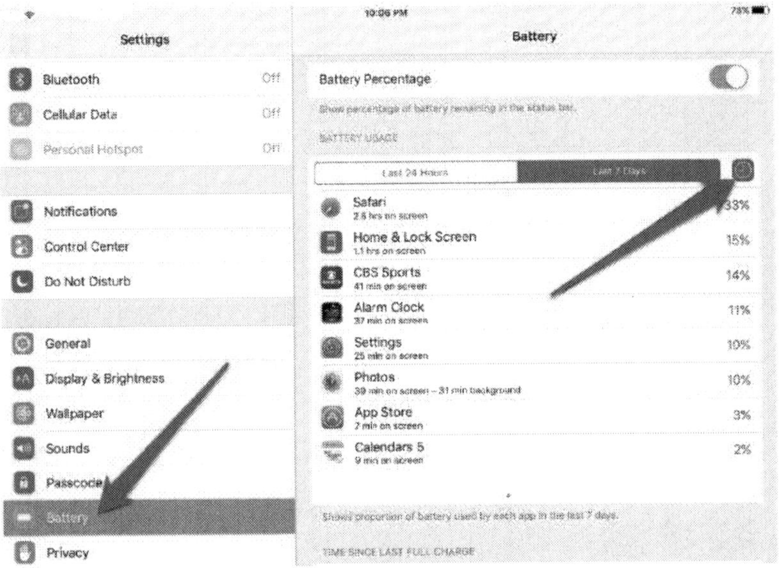

Get familiar with the Battery and Screentime Chat. It shows you a great break down of your battery life and what applications are using most of your battery life. You can get precise battery usage by clicking on the bar chat at specific hours. You could also get an average of battery usage by apps over the last ten days.

- Go to "Settings
- Tap on "Battery"

Screen Time

Screen time empowers users with both insight and control over how they spend their time. It is a useful tool that allows you to regulate your iPad usage. Screen time starts with Report; every week, you get a weekly activity summary with details of how you used your iPad. You see what apps you have used, how long you have used them, how many times you have picked up your iPad etc. You also see several data points like the most used app and also set time for the iPad to shutdown. When you set those time up, your iPad automatically alerts you when you have reached your usage time limit. You can also set daily limits for different app categories. There is also an "always allow" section that allows you to "whitelist" some apps. The iPad app is white-listed by default to enable people call out in case of an emergency.

Screen Time Widget

You can enable the screen time widget to go along the new screen time preferences with the iPad Pro. With this, you have quick glanceable access to some of your high-level device usage statistics. You can also go to the full-screen time section of the preferences by simply tapping on the widget.

How to Use Downtime in Screen Time

Downtime allows you schedule time away from your screen, to activate it;

- Open Settings
- Tap Screen Time
- Tap Downtime and toggle the switch ON.
- Next, choose a start and end time. During down time, all apps and notifications will

be blocked. But you will still have access to calls and apps on your allowed apps list.

- When you are done with the changes, tap "Screen Time" to go back.
- You can choose always allowed apps by Tapping the "Always Allowed ". Here you will see a list of important apps you can still use during downtimes like phone, messages, FaceTime and Maps. If you want to remove an app from the list of "Always Allowed" apps, tap to remove an app.
- To add an app to the "Always Allowed", scroll down and tap the green plus sign next to the app you wish to allow.
- Tap "Back" when done making changes to your list. Now you are ready for downtime

When Downtime is active, the home screen dims all blocked apps and you will see an hour-glass icon next to the app. You will still receive notifications from the apps on your "Always Allowed" list but not from other apps. You can use a passcode to get into the Screen time settings which you would want to do if you have kids you are a little bit older or smarter enough to figure out how to disable some of the screen time features.

How to bypass Downtime Limits

If you try to open an app when it is unavailable, you will see a time limit warning. You can still use the app. Tap "Ignore Limit".

- Then tap "Remind Me in 15 Minutes" to snooze. This allows you use the app for a little while.
- Tap "Ignore Limit For Today" to completely unlock it.
- You can tap "Cancel" to accept limit and move on.

How to Automatically hide the Pointer

You can change auto-hide settings for the pointer. By default, the pointer auto hides after 2 seconds of non-use. However, you can increase this time by going to 'Settings' > 'Accessibility' > Under 'Pointer and Control' click on 'Automatically hide pointer.' Here you can increase the timing for pointer auto-hide. The highest time allowed is fifteen seconds, which means if the iPad pro mouse or trackpad remains untouched for the number of seconds you select, the pointer disappears from the screen. Note that you can also disable auto-hide to allow the pointer to stay on the screen.

How to change Pointer Color

The iPad Pro's Pointer outline colors can be changed to aid its visibility. To do this, go to 'Settings'> 'Accessibility'> 'Pointer and Control' and click on 'Color.' Here you can customize the outline of the pointer by selecting any of the listed colors (white, blue, red, green, yellow, orange). You can also change the size of the stroke by increasing the stroke size slider.

How to Increase Pointer Size

You may want to increase the size of the pointer due to visual impairment or any other reason. To do this, go to 'Setting > 'Accessibility' > 'Pointer and Control' > and slide over the 'Pointer Size' slide bar.

How to disable Pointer animations

By default, when you mouse over a button or an icon, the pointer disappears into that button or icon, making it a little bit hard to discern where the pointer is as a result. But you can disable this animation so that the pointer always remains visible even when they placed over a button or an icon. To do this, go to

'Settings' > 'Accessibility' > 'Pointer and Control' > and disable 'Pointer Animations'.

How to change scrolling speed

You can change the scroll speed on a list or safari by either increasing the velocity or reducing it with each swipe. To do this, go to 'Settings'> 'Accessibility'> 'Pointer and Controls'> move the Scrolling speed slider between the tortoise and the mice. Slide it to the left towards the tortoise to decrease the scrolling speed and to the right towards the mice to increase the scrolling speed.

Configure Notifications

Configure all of your notifications so you won't get barrage of notifications from every single applications. Notifications are little reminders that show up on your screen when apps want your attention. When someone sends you a text message for instance, and a badge appears on your screen, that is a notification. Setting up a notification ensures you see only the ones you care about and allow you control how they appear on your iPad. This way you don't get overwhelmed with notifications you don't care about.

To set up notifications,

- Open your "SETTINGS" app
- Tap on "Notifications"
- The next screen shows you all the apps that can send you notifications and you can control the settings for each one of them.
- For this example, let's choose how we want to receive text messages notification.
- Scroll down and tap on "Messages."
- "Allow notifications" let you decide if you want to receive notifications at all. If you don't want any form of notifications from

any app, tap the white circle, so the green goes away. That way, you have DISABLED notification for that particular app.

- The "Show in notification Center" option when toggled ON allows notifications from that app to be displayed in the notification center. You can access the notification center by swiping from top down on the home screen and a list of all your recent notifications will appear. This could be missed calls, an upcoming calendar event etc.
- The next option you can customize is "Sound". Select it and a large list of sound is displayed. You can click through them and pre-hear each one until you find the one you prefer.
- After choosing a sound, tap "messages" in the top left to return to the notification menu.

- The next option helps you choose the style of notification. The first option is the badge. This notification puts a small red number  on your app icon on the home screen. This number tells you how many notifications in this app are waiting for you.

[[

- The second option is "Show on lock screen". When this is turned ON, notifications will show up on your lock screen.

Finally, you can choose your notification style, when your iPad is unlocked. The first option is "None". This will prevent any form of notification from showing up on your screen while you use the iPad. The second option is "Banner". A Banner will appear at the top of your screen and then disappear after a few seconds. The third option is "Alerts". This puts a banner at the top of your screen that won't go away until you take action.

At the bottom of the notification settings menu are two more options specific to the messages app. If you want to read some of the messages within the notification banner, tap "Show Preview" and then select "Always" or "When Unlocked". If you don't want to see the content of the message until you open it, select "OFF".

Finally, you can choose to repeat alerts, if you want to be reminded continously. You can control the notifications for individual apps by going into each of them in the notification setting and Disable or Enable each. Activating several app notifications will drain your iPad batteries.

Notification Grouping

Notifications "by App" allow you group notification together to appear as a bubble.

iCloud

How to increase iCloud Storage

Consider upgrading your iPad storage plan to make room for other things such as images, movies and applications. You can expand your storage by up to 200GB for just $2.99 a month.

- Go to "Settings"
- Tap on your Apple profile
- Tap on iCloud
- Tap on "Manage storage" › tap "Change Storage plan". This takes you to a screen

which allows you to purchase more storage. You can get up to 2TB for $9.99 a month. Tap on the option that suits your storage need and hit the "Buy" button.

How to have backups to your Photos on iCloud

There are a couple of things you can tweak on the photo library and one of them is to enable iCloud photo library. You get 5GB of storage with every iPhone you purchase. To ensure all your photos and videos are backed up to the iCloud,

- Go to Settings
- Tap on Photos
- Enable iCloud Photo Library.

Charging your iPhone from your iPad Pro

You can use the iPad pro as a power bank to charge other devices (e.g iPhone) when they are low on battery with the aid of a USB-C-to-

Lightning cable. Connect the USB-C-to-lightning cable to the iPhone and the iPad Pro. The Lightning end goes into the iPhone lightning port and the USB-C end goes into the iPad Pro USB-C port. This is a great way to charge your iPhone if there is no charging outlet close by or if you don't have a portable charger.

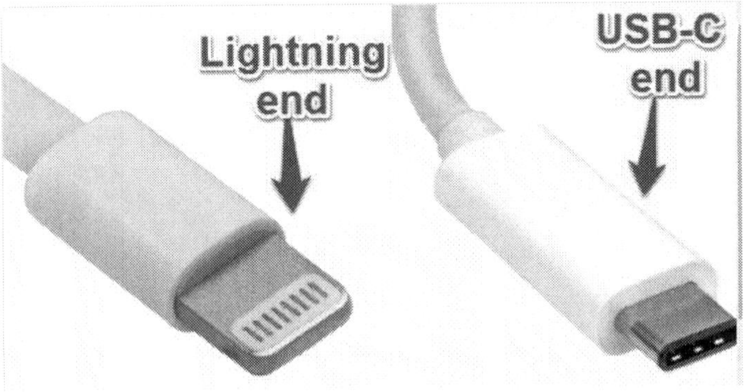

USB-C to lightning cable

Adding Virtual Home Button

Although the iPad Pro does not have the home button, you can activate a virtual home button by going to

- Settings
- "Accessibility"

- "Touch"
- Scroll down to "Assistive touch" and turn it ON. This will bring up the Assistive Touch on the screen.
- Tap on the icon to display several icons such as Control Center, screenshot, Device, Home, Lock Screen, volume up/Down, screen lock, Siri etc. You can change the assistive touch button to play the role of only a Home button by going to:
- Settings
- "Accessibility"
- "Touch"
- "Assistive touch"
- Then tap on "Customize". Take away all the assistive touch button and tap on the "favorite" icon with the pencil, Scroll down the dialogue box to add a custom button. This time it would be "Home" and the assistive touch button becomes a Home

button solely. Tap on the button while in any app and it takes you to the Home Screen. This button can be placed anywhere on the screen and does not interfere with your access to iPad pro features and apps. It is a great tool for those that want the Home button back.

Transfering Media from Gopro to iPad Pro.

Plug one end of the USB-C cord that came with the iPad pro into the GoPro and the other end directly into the USB-C port of the iPad. It pops up the "Import" tool to transfer the media from the GoPro over to the iPad.

Connecting the Old iPhone to the iPad Pro

You can transfer media directly from one old iPad/iPhone device to another. You can do this with the aid of a lightning-to-USB cable.

- Plug in the USB-C end to the iPad Pro and the lightning end to any iPad or iPhone.
- It requests that you "allow the connection" > click on "Allow" and you will have access to all the media on the iPad Pro.

Using Night Shift

This is a feature that automatically adjusts the colors on your iPad Pro display to the warmer end of the spectrum, making the display easy on your eyes. To toggle ON night shift, go to Settings > Display & Brightness > Night shift. You can also automatically schedule night shift to turn ON and adjust the color temperature at specific times of the day.

Make Your iPad Pro Speak

This is an accessibility feature that allows the iPad Pro to read out what is on its screen and selected text. It is a handy feature for iPad Pro users with visual impairment. To set this up, go to Settings › tap 'Accessibility' › 'Spoken Content' and enable any of the following

- Speak Selection: To hear the text you selected, tap the Speak button.
- Speak Screen: To hear the entire screen, swipe down with two fingers from the top of the screen.
- Speech Controller: Show the controller for quick access to Speak Screen and Speak on Touch.
- Highlight Content: The iPad can highlight words, sentences, or both as they're spoken. You can change the highlight color and style.
- Typing Feedback: You can configure typing feedback for the onscreen and external keyboards and choose to have iPad speak each character, entire words, auto-

corrections, auto-capitalizations, and typing predictions.

- To hear typing predictions, you also need to go to Settings > General > Keyboards, then turn on Predictive.
- Voices: Choose a voice and dialect.
- Speaking Rate: Drag the slider.
- Pronunciations: Dictate or spell out how you want specific phrases to be Pronounced.

Audio Description

Audio description is another accessibility feature, and it allows users to have access to audio and subtitles for movies or videos that includes audio description or subtitle. If you want videos to use audio description by default, go to settings > accessibility > tap 'Audio description' and turn it ON.

You can control other Apple devices on the same Wi-Fi network remotely from the iPad Pro using 'Switch Control.' Switch control allows you you MAC, Apple TV, iPhone or any other Apple Device. To use switch control, connect all devices to the same Wi-Fi network › sign in to iCloud on the device using the same Apple ID › If you want to control a Mac, choose Apple menu › System Preferences on your computer. Select Accessibility. In the sidebar, select Control Switch. Check the checkbox next to "Allow platform switching to control your computer." If you haven't already, turn on Switch Control on your iPad. Use your switch to navigate the Switch Control Menu. Select Device› Select Use Other Device › Select the Device that you want to control, then select Connect. Now you can use the switch connected to your iPad to control the other Device.

Control Your iPad With Voice

You can navigate through and interact with your iPad Pro via voice control. You can type, tap, swipe, click, and do more on the iPad using voice control. To turn ON voice control, go to 'Settings' > select 'Accessibility' > select 'Voice Control' > this will trigger a file download > when the download is complete, a microphone icon appears on the status bar which indicates when the voice control is listening or not.

When Voice Control is Enabled, you can speak commands like you would when performing a touch gesture. For example, to access Spotlight Search on the Home screen, say, "Swipe down." Or to access long-press menus for certain apps, say "Long press [app name]." Voice Control doesn't change how your device responds to touch. To have access to a list of available commands for different situations, say, "Show me what to say." To view the full list of commands, you can use these steps: Go to 'Settings' > select 'Accessibility' > Select 'Voice Control,' > then Customize Commands.

To interact with items on your screen, say an action, such as "Tap," then say the name of the menu or item you want to tap. For example, say "Tap Accessibility." If you're not sure what the name of the menu or item is, you can say, "Show names" to display an overlay with the item names. If an item doesn't have a name, or if you would prefer to use numbers instead, you can say, "Show Numbers" to display numeric tags for each item on your screen.

For interactions that require more precision, you can say, "Show grid" to display a numbered grid lines overlay with numbers for each cell. Speaking a number on the grid will enlarge that area of the grid and present a new set of numbers, which will make it easier for you to select an item or section of the grid overlay. The grid can also be used when dragging items on the screen to identify where you would like to drop them, or when performing gesture or freehand actions. After speaking your next command, the grid will disappear. To keep the grid on screen for multiple commands, say "Show grid continuously."

How to Reduce Transperency

The 'Reduce transparency' setting, reduces transparency and blurs in some backgrounds by increasing contrast. This setting enhances the legibility of text by altering text color and style. To turn ON 'Reduced transparency,' go to 'Settings' > Accessibility' > 'Display and Text Size' and turn ON 'Reduce Transparency.'

Under the 'Display & Text Size' Menu, there are other options that improve text readability, and this includes Bold text, larger text, increase contrast, smart invert, classic invert, etc.

Chapter 6

Siri

Siri has been around for a while, but it is easy to forget the basics of Siri commands. A lot can be done with Siri on the iPad Pro. To activate Siri on the iPad Pro, go to 'Settings' > tap 'Siri & Search' > turn Siri ON. Siri is activated by saying "Hey! Siri", followed by your request. Alternatively, you can press and hold the top button to activate Siri.

The list of Siri commands continues to grow and evolve with the continuous improvements and addition of new Siri commands. These new improvements in the voice recognition Artificial Intelligence Technology is geared towards making iPad Pro users get better and more efficient ways to communicate with the iPad using natural language. However, you can try new commands and don't have to say it exactly the way you see them in this manual. The list below is not exhaustive because new phrases are continuously being added to the Siri voice command.

Basic Siri Commands

- List things you can ask Siri: {Hey Siri, what can I ask you?}
- When asking Siri for help: {"Hey Siri, help."}
- Getting into a conversation with Siri: (Hey Siri, let's chat."}
- Changing Volume on the watch: {"Hey Siri, set the volume to 5," "Hey Siri, louder" or "Hey Siri, turn up/down the volume."}
- Display photos: {"Hey Siri, show my photos" or, "Hey Siri, show me pictures of cats."}
- Ask the Siri to display the weather forecast: {"Hey Siri, show me the weekend forecast."}

- Ask Siri to display food recipes: {"Hey Siri, show me a slow cooker recipe."}
- Ask Siri to Send a text Message {Hey Siri, send a text message to Michael} then dictate the text message to be sent to Michael.
- Ask Siri to change a text Message (Hey Sir, Change it)
- Ask Siri to add more text to a message (Hey Siri, add to it)
- Instructing the Siri to display timers: {"Hey Siri, show me my timers."}
- Use the Siri to open app: {"Hey Siri, open Uber."}
- Opening stored apps: {"Hey Siri, open [app name] " or "Hey Siri, launch [app name]"}
- Return Watch to home screen: {"Hey Siri, ret-urn home."}
- Call someone on speaker mode: {Hey Siri, call Maxwell on speaker."}

- Find out distance: {"Hey Siri, how far away is Chicago?"}
- Play Voicemail recording:{"Hey Siri, play my last voicemail"}
- Ask for Stock price: {Hey Siri, what's the Apple stock at"}
- Read text messages: {Hey Siri, read my last text message from Maxwell"}
- Send text messages: {Hey Siri, text mum saying we are on our way"}
- Know your exact location:{Hey Siri, where am i?"}
- Temperature conversion:{Hey Siri, what 75° in Fahrenheit"}
- Ask Siri to read your notifications {Hey Siri, Read my notifications}
- Ask Siri to find your airpod or Apple Watch {Hey Siri, find my airpods or find my Apple Watch}

- Ask Siri to show your QR Code for your twitter account so you can share it with others {Hey Siri, twitter QR Code}
- Ask Siri For the email address of any of your contact {Hey Siri, what is the email address of John}
- Ask Siri to scan a QR Code {Hey Siri, Scan a QR code}
- Ask Siri to remember a website while you are on the site {Hey Siri, remember this}
- Ask Siri to Call a contact on speaker {Hey Siri, call Andrew on speaker}
- Ask Siri to open the settings while using an app {Hey Siri, preferences}
- Ask Siri to turn ON low power mode {Hey Siri, low power mode ON}
- Ask Siri to check if any of your settings is turned ON or OFF {Hey Siri, is Bluetooth ON?}

- Ask Siri to install an app without going to the app store {Hey Siri, Install Netflix}
- Ask Siri to read mail from a particular contact {Read Emails from Andrew}

Siri Translation

Hey Siri, translate "What time is it" to French
Hey Siri, say "this food is delicious" in Mandarin
Hey Siri, say "I Love you" in Spanish

Siri Media controls

- Siri command to play music: {"Hey Siri, play some music."}
- Place specific song or artist on a queue: {"Hey Siri, play music by [artist]."}
- Playing songs based on content: {"Hey Siri, play the latest Avett Brothers album" or "Hey Siri, play that song that goes 'Gotta gotta be down, because I want it all.'"}

- Playing music based on a theme: {"Hey Siri, play baby making music" or "Hey Siri, play rock music for working."}
- Playing the song of the day: {"Hey Siri, play the song of the day."}
- Set a timer for sleep: {"Hey Siri set a sleep timer for 45 minutes" or Hey Siri, stop playing in 45 minutes."}
- Get detail information about a song: {"Hey Siri, what's playing?"}
- Control Music: {"Hey Siri, play" or "Hey Siri, next."}
- Restart a song: {"Hey Siri, restart."}

Siri Time and date

- Setting an alarm: {"Hey Siri, set an alarm for 7 a.m." or "Hey Siri, wake me up at 7 in the morning."}
- Setting a music alarm: {"Hey Siri, wake me up to [artist, song, genre, playlist or album] at 8

a.m.," "Hey Siri, set an alarm to Band of Horses" or "Hey Siri, wake me up to Kiss FM on TuneIn."}

- Setting a repeating alarm: {"Hey Siri, set a repeating alarm for weekdays at 7 a.m."}
- Setting a timer: {"Hey Siri, timer" or "Hey Siri, set a timer for 15 minutes."}
- Create timer with a name: {"Hey Siri, set a pizza timer for 20 minutes."}
- Setting multiple timers: {"Hey Siri, set a second timer for 5 minutes."}
- Check timer status: {"Hey Siri, how much time is left on the pizza timer?" or "Hey Siri, what are my timers?"}
- Cancelling a timer: {"Hey Siri, cancel the pizza timer" or "Hey Siri, cancel the 15 minute timer."}
- Ask for time: {"Hey Siri, what time is it?"}
- Ask for date: {"Hey Siri, what's the date?"}

- Cancel an alarm: {"Hey Siri, cancel my alarm for 3 p.m."}
- Snooze alarm: {"Hey Siri, snooze."}
- Check dates: {"Hey Siri, when is [holiday] this year?"}

Siri To-do and shopping lists

- Add task to to-do list {"Hey Siri, add "go to the grocery store" to my to-do list" or "Hey Siri, I need to make an appointment with the doctor."}
- Create a new to-do item: {"Hey Siri, create a to-do."}
- Check events on calendar: {"Hey Siri, what's on my calendar for tomorrow?"}
- Scan QR Code: {Scan a QR code"}
- Add an event to calendar: {"Hey Siri, add [event] to my calendar for [day] at [time]" or "Hey Siri, add an event to my calendar."}

- Create a shopping list: {"Hey Siri, add eggs to my shopping list" or "Hey Siri, I need to buy laundry detergent."}
- Check shopping list: {"Hey Siri, what's on my shopping list?"}
- Create a reminder: {"Hey Siri, reminder" or "Hey Siri, remind me to check the oven in 5 minutes."} {"Hey Siri, remind me to pay my bills tomorrow"}
- Check existing reminders: {"Hey Siri, what are my reminders this weekend?" or "Hey Siri, what reminders do I have tomorrow?"}

Siri News and Weather

- Check News headlines: {"Hey Siri, what's in the news?"}
- Check the weather: {"Hey Siri, what's the weather like?" or "Hey Siri, will it rain today?" You can also ask " Hey Siri, will I need an umbrella today?"}

- Get weather forecast: {"Hey Siri, what's the weather going to be like this weekend?}
- Get update on traffic situation: {"Hey Siri, what's my commute look like?" or "Hey Siri, what's traffic like?"}

Siri Entertainment

- Search for movies to be screened at a near-by theaters: {"Hey Siri, what movies are playing?" or "Hey Siri, what action movies are playing tonight?"}
- Get information on movies playing: {"Hey Siri, tell me about the movie [title]."}
- Get movie quotes: {"Hey Siri, give me a [movie] quote."}

Get IMDb rating: {"Hey Siri, what is the IMDb rating for [movie or TV show]?"}
- Get cast for a movie or show: {"Hey Siri, who plays in [movie or TV show]?"}
- Find out who an actor is: {"Hey Siri, who played [character] in [movie or TV show]?"}

- Find an actor's recent works: Hey Siri, what is [actor]'s latest movie?"}
- Find out who sang a song playing on your device or at random: {"Hey Siri, who sang the song [title]?"}
- Get the names of a musical band members: {"Hey Siri, who is in the band [name]?"}
- Get music album information: {"Hey Siri, what year did [band] release [song or album]?"}
- Find popular music by an artist: {"Hey Siri, what's popular from [artist]?"}
- Find sample music from an artist: {"Hey Siri, sample songs by [artist]."}
- Find an album or song: {"Hey Siri, find [song or album] by [artist]."}
- Scroll Left or Right: {"Hey Siri, scroll left or Hey Siri Scroll Right}
- Show available seasons of movies: {Hey Siri show me seasons"}

Siri Food and Businesses

- Get food recipes: Hey Siri, how do you make chocolate chip cookies?"} {Hey Siri, create a grocery list"}
- Locate a nearby restaurant: {"Hey Siri, find me a nearby pizza restaurant" or "Hey Siri, what's the nearest coffee shop?"}
- Get operating hours or a phone number for local businesses: {"Hey Siri, find the address for Bank of America" or "Hey Siri, find business hours for McDonald."}
- Get recipes for a meal Hey Siri, what ingredients are in a Reuben sandwich"}

Siri Calculations/Conversions

- Convert units: {"Hey Siri, how many [units] are in [units]?"} {Hey Siri, how many ounces are in a gallon?"}
- Convert units: {"Hey Siri, how many [units] are in 2 [units]?"}

- Basic mathematics: {"Hey Siri, what's 5 plus 7?" or Hey Siri, what's 56 times 33?"}
- Advanced mathematics: {"Hey Siri, 70 factorials."}

Siri Definitions and Spellings

- Get the definition of a word:{"Hey Siri,what's the definition of [word]?"}
- Get the spelling of a word: {"Hey Siri, how do you spell [word]?"}

Siri Sports

- Check the results of a finished game: Hey Siri, what was the score of the [team] game?"}
- Ask if a team won a game: {"Hey Siri, did the [team] win?"}
- Ask when a team's next game is scheduled: {"Hey Siri, when do the [team] play next?"}
- Find out the results of your favorite teams: {"Hey Siri, give me my Sports Update."}

- Get Fantasy Football update with the Yahoo Fantasy Football skill: {"Hey Siri, ask Yahoo Fantasy Football for a score update " or" Hey Siri, ask Yahoo Fantasy Football if Colin Kaepernick is playing this week."}
- Get league standings of all teams: {"Hey Siri, what are the MLB standings?"}

Siri Searches

- Get information on Wikipedia: {"Hey Siri, Wikipedia: [subject]."}
- Tell Siri to continue reading a Wikipedia entry: {"Hey Siri, tell me more."}
- Ask Siri a general question: {"Hey Siri, how tall is [person or object's name]?"}
- Ask a general question: {"Hey Siri, how many people live in America?"}
- Get a "Game of Thrones" quote: {"Hey Siri, give me a 'Game of Thrones' quote."}

- Search for Photos: Enable Siri and Search to be able to ask Siri to search for photos. Tap on Settings > "Siri Search" > Enable "Search & Siri Suggestions" {Hey Siri, show me the photos that were taken today."}
- Search for Apps: {Hey Siri, search the App Store for the best free games"}

Siri Voice

The iPadOS 13.4 has given users the ability to control the iPad completely using voice. To enable this feature, go to settings > Accessibility > Voice control > and turn it ON. You can also do this using voice control using the command {Hey Siri, turn ON voice control}.

Siri Holidays

- Find out when a holiday is: {"Hey Siri, when is [holiday]?"}

- Holiday limerick: {"Hey Siri, tell me a holiday limerick."}
- Learn about a holiday: {"Hey Siri, why do we celebrate [holiday]?"}
- Ask about Santa: {"Hey Siri, how old is Santa Claus?" "Hey Siri, is Santa Claus real?" or "Hey Siri, where does Santa Claus live?"}
- Ask about Santa's reindeer: {"Hey Siri, who's your favorite reindeer?" "Hey Siri, what can you tell me about Santa's reindeer?" or "Hey Siri, what do you know about Rudolph the rednosed reindeer?"}
- Track Santa: {"Hey Siri, where is Santa?" or "Hey Siri, track Santa."}
- Sing a Christmas carol: {"Hey Siri, sing a Christmas carol."}
- Have Siri read "The Night Before Christmas": {"Hey Siri, read "The Night Before Christmas."}
- Spin the dreidel: {"Hey Siri, spin the dreidel."}

- Ask for holiday jokes:{"Hey Siri, open my gift," "Hey Siri, how ugly is your/my holiday sweater?" or "Hey Siri, tell me a snowman joke."}
- Ask for holiday movies?:{"Hey Siri, what's your favorite holiday movie?" or "Hey Siri, what are the top holiday movies?"}

Siri Shortcuts

Siri shortcuts allow Siri to carry out multiple actions with only one command. This is only possible if you have the Siri shortcut App installed in your iPad.

- Open the Siri Shortcut App on your iPad.
- At the home screen of the Siri Shortcut App is the library where you find a list of Siri shortcuts and "Create Shortcuts."
- Click on "Create shortcut" to create your shortcut. Let say you want your Alarm to go off at a certain time, and you need it to play music at the same time. What you do

is search for the Clock App Set, the time for the Alarm at 5.00am. Next search for the Music App, and select the music of your choice. Let's say you also want the screen brightness reduced when the alarm goes off. Search for the "Set Brightness" and dim the brightness. Also, you may want to set your "do not disturb" to automatically turn ON when the alarm goes OFF. So that when the Alarm clock goes off, it will start playing music, the screen brightness becomes dim, and "Do Not Disturb" will be deactivated.

- To bring you to another list of options, tap on the "switch icon" on the top right corner and from here you can rename your icon, preset your Siri recording, that is you can say a certain phrase and that phrase will launch the shortcut you just created. For instance, you could name the shortcut "In the Morning." So when you say "Hey Siri, In the Morning". This will automatically set the Clock alarm to 5.00am and when the alarm goes off, your iPad will play a piece of pre-selected music, it also dims screen brightness and switches Off "Do Not Disturb". Click on "Done" to finish the Siri Shortcut setup.

- You could also use Siri Shortcut to carryout a list of activities when you are about to board an airplane, instead of going through each of the options that are not permitted for flight and deactivating them.

There is no limit to the list of activities that can be done with Siri Shortcut. These shortcuts can be launched on the Home screen, widget panel and they can also be edited. If you want to edit a shortcut, go into the shortcut app, tap on the three ellipses, tap on the settings you wish to change.

Chapter 7

Troubleshooting the iPad Pro

iPad Pro Won't Turn ON

When your iPad refuses to turn ON, it is either a Software or Hardware problem. The first thing you should do is to troubleshoot the software. A software crash can prevent the iPad Pro from powering ON.

Solution: The way out is to force reset the iPad. This is done by pressing and holding the VOLUME UP, VOLUME DOWN and the POWER buttons simultaneously for 10 - 15 seconds and this will force reset the iPad Pro. This action completely shuts down the iPad. Alternatively, you can reset the iPad by the following action - press and quickly release the volume up button, press and quickly release the volume down button and then press and hold the side button until you see the Apple logo. You should only use forced reset when you encounter a glitch while operating your iPad and you can't power OFF the iPad by default.

If after carrying out a forced reset on your iPad and the glitch goes away, then continue using the iPad. But if the software glitch keeps happening over and over again, you will need to carry reset "All Settings." This is a sort of non-invasive software fix because it resets everything in the settings App but does not affect any of your personal information. To do this,

- Go to the "Settings" App
- Tap "General"
- Scroll down and tap "Reset."
- Tap on "Reset All Settings"
- Enter your passcode and tap "Reset All Settings" to confirm. Reset will take place

and iPad will restart. This will fix your software glitch problems.

If the above does not work and you are still having a software issue, then you will need to do a DFU Restore. DFU Restore is the last ditch effort to fix any software problem on the iPad. If a software fix is going to work, then the DFU Restore is the way to go.

Fix Software Glitch using DFU Restore

This is the deepest kind of restore you can do on the iPad. If there is a software problem with your iPad, DFU restore will probably fix it. Highlighted below are steps for DFU Restore :

- Plug your iPad into a computer running iTunes
- A dialogue box pops up on the computer requesting to access your iPad, click "NO." iTunes in this respect is not transferring

any data. It is just a tool to DFU restore your iPad.

- Hold down the VOLUME UP, VOLUME DOWN and the Power buttons simultaneously until the screen turns black or until the Apple logo appears and disappears.
- Continue holding on the side button until the computer detects your iPad in recovery mode. Click "OK" on the dialogue box that pops up on the screen.
- Click on the "Restore and Update" button that pops up on the computer screen. This will download the latest version of iPadOS automatically and load it to the iPad.
- Note: Always backup your iPad before putting it to DFU mode.

If the DFU restore doesn't work, then the problem is Hardware related.

Solution: Check the charging port at the bottom of the iPad. Dust or other debris could get into the charging port and prevent the USB-C cable terminals from contacting properly. You can get a toothbrush you have never used before or antiasthenic brush to brush off the debris within the port. If this step doesn't solve it, the next port of call is the USB-C cable and the iPad charger. Ensure they are both in perfect working condition or needs replacement. Try it out with other devices that use USB-C cable. If this still does not solve it, plug your iPad Pro to a computer to see if the computer will recognize it on iTunes. If it is, then it could be a display issue and not an overall hardware issue. If it is recognized by iTune, quickly backup your iPad so you don't loss your information in case things get worse. Then send your iPad for repairs.

iPad Pro Screen is Frozen

Several factors could result in frozen iPad scr-een.

Solution:Frozen screen can be resolved by hard reset. Hold down the VOLUME UP, VOLUME DOWN and the Power buttons simultaneously until the screen turns black or until the Apple logo appears and disappears.

iPad Won't Charge

If your iPad doesn't charge, it could either be software or a hardware problem. But it is impo-rtant to start by troubleshooting the software.

Solution: Hard reset your iPad by holding down the VOLUME UP, VOLUME DOWN and the Power buttons simultaneously for 10 - 15 sec-onds until the Apple logo appears. A lot of the time when an iPad refuses to charge, it is as a result of a software crash. If this does not work, look at the iPad cable for frames and discoloration. Try different cable and chargers. If this does not resolve it, clean up the charging port. If this still does not resolve it, do a DFU reset. Finally, if the DFU reset does not fix it, then take it for repairs.

Pencil Won't Write or Draw Properly

Solution: Make sure the end of the pencil is properly screwed. If after screwing the tip of the pencil and problem persists, reset the iPad.

Smart Keyboard is unresponsive

When this problem occurs, users find it difficult to type when they enter a text field on the iPad. Most times the text field is waiting for input and the software keyboard is displayed on the screen but the smart keyboard is unresponsive. Most often than not, what results in keyboard not responding in an iPad is because the keypad is not sitting properly, preventing the terminals from making proper contact with the iPad even though the magnetic field is strong.

Solution: To solve this problem, slide the keyboard one way or the other. When you do this, you will notice that the software keyboard will disappear from the screen when contact is made.

Cannot Connect to App Store

Inability to connect your iPad Pro to the App store is a common problem with iPads.

Solution: Ensure the device is connected to a Wifi Connection.

- Go to "Setting"
- Select "iTunes App store"
- Toggle ON "Apps" and "Updates"
- Go back to the Setting menu and Select "General."
- Select "Date Time" and Turn OFF "Set Automatically"

- Select your Region or City and ensure the time is correct
- Go back and select "Reset."
- Reset only the "Network and Wifi Setting."
- Wait for the device to reboot
- Reconfigure your Wifi connection by going back to "settings" and select "Wifi Conne-ction."
- Enter the Wifi password
- Go back to the Menu Screen and select "App store". This should resolve the problem with your iPad Pro not connecting to the Apple App Store.

iPad Screen won't rotate

This is a software issue and rarely a hardware problem. Most times your iPad screen won't rotate because device orientation lock is turned ON. You can set orientation lock to either landscape mode or portrait mode on the iPad without knowing. There are couple of ways to turn this OFF. First is through the control center.

- Swipe down the top right corner of your screen to open the control center
- Locate the device orientation lock button 
- Tap the button to turn device Orientation lock OFF.

If the device orientation lock is OFF and the iPad won't rotate, then the device orientation App is crashed and need to be closed.

- Go to "Settings"
- Tap on "General"
- Scroll down to "Reset" and tap on "Reset All Settings"
- Enter your passcode
- After resetting, reconfigure the Wifi sett-ings and this should solve it.

You can find a lost or stolen iPad with the aid of the "Find my iPad/iPhone" feature on your device. If you don't have this App on your iPad, you can install it. To turn ON the "Find my iPad" feature;

- Go to "Settings"
- Scroll down and tap on "iCloud" to bring up a menu on the right.
- Locate the "Find My iPad" feature and toggle it ON.

If you get your device lost or stolen, here are the steps to recover it using iCloud;

- Visit iCloud.com

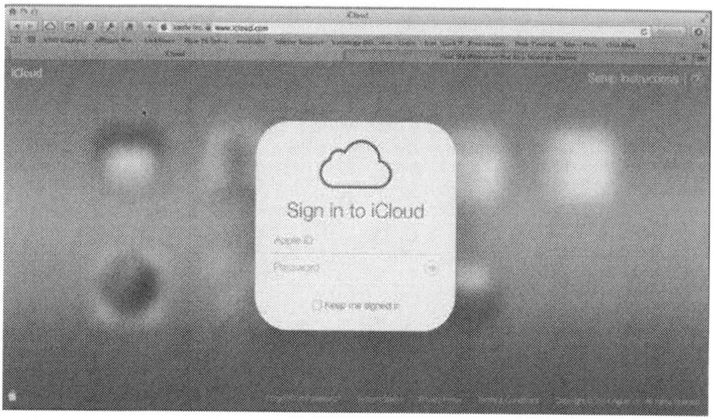

- log into your iCloud Account

- Click on the "Find My iPhone" icon.
- At the top of the screen, you will find a drop down Menu with the tag "All Devices", tap on it to see all of the devices that are connected to your iCloud account and tap the device you wish to find.
- Choose the iPad Proofrom the list of devices to be located.
- The green button on the map indicates the exact location of the missing iPad.

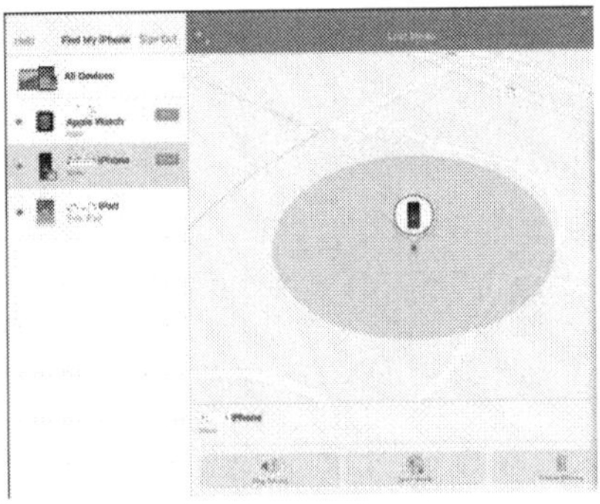

- Zoom in as much as you want on the location to see the exact location of the device.
- If it is within the house and wasn't stolen but misplaced, Click on the "Play Sound" button. This will activate a sound on the device so you can locate it.
- If you cannot locate the device because it is not connected to Wifi, Click on "Lost mode" or choose to "Erase iPad" ensuring to ensure that no one else has access to your files or wallet. If you backed up your device before it got stolen or missing, it would be restored in your new device when you sync it to your iCloud.
- When you click on "Lost Mode" you will be requested to enter a phone number where you can be reached. This number will be shown on your missing iPad. If you don't have a passcode setup on the iPad before

it got missing, you will be requested to enter a passcode to lock the iPad.

- After keying in the phone number, click "Next" to take you to a message box where you are to enter a message that will be shown with your phone number on your stolen or missing iPad. The default message is "This iPad has been lost, Please Call me." You can change it to whatever message you prefer. Unless the passcode is known, the iPad is useless to anyone who has it. Click on "Done" when you are done typing the message.
- If you don't like the map, you can change it to standard, satellite or Hybrid mode at the bottom left side of the screen.

About the Author

Derrick Richard is a tech geek with several years of experience in the ICT industry. He passionately follows latest tech trends and his passion is in figuring out the solution to complex problems.

Derrick holds a Bachelor and a Master's Degree in ICT respectively from Georgetown University, Washington DC. He lives in Sarasota, Florida.

Printed in Poland
by Amazon Fulfillment
Poland Sp. z o.o., Wrocław

58961863R00132